"*Civil Society, Care Labour, and the Women, Peace and Security Agenda: Making 1325 Work* addresses an urgent gap in the literature by placing centre stage the unpaid care work of those engaged in making change happen within the WPS framework in contexts of underfunding and austerity. This brings into focus a political economy lens to show us the importance and costs of this labour done under difficult circumstances by thousands of committed civil society actors in the public and the domestic spheres. By recognising the subsidy that this social reproductive labour provides to the global WPS regime, the authors chart an agenda for change within the WPS system."

— Shirin Rai,
Professor of Politics and International Studies and Director of the Warwick Interdisciplinary Research Centre for International Development, University of Warwick, UK

"Caitlin Hamilton, Anuradha Mundkur and Laura J. Shepherd eloquently articulate and explore a question at the heart of the Women, Peace and Security agenda: how has it come so far, given its chronic underfunding? Through a brilliant analysis that recognizes and amplifies the perspectives of women peacebuilders, this book sheds light on peacebuilding as a form of care labor, and opens up exciting new directions for research and policy. It is an important contribution to the urgent call to adequately fund work of women peacebuilders!"

— Agnieszka Fal-Dutra Santos,
Program Coordinator and Peacebuilding Policy Specialist, Global Network of Women Peacebuilders

Civil Society, Care Labour, and the Women, Peace and Security Agenda

This book proposes that work on the Women, Peace and Security agenda undertaken by civil society actors can be interpreted as a form of care labour that nourishes and sustains the agenda – without which the agenda could not, in fact, succeed. The care labour of civil society is thus a condition of the Women, Peace and Security agenda's success.

United Nations Security Council resolution 1325 is the foundation of a diverse and pluralising policy framework known as the Women, Peace and Security agenda. Over the 20 years since the adoption of the foundational resolution, despite sustained resistance from some quarters and a general lack of adequate resourcing and political will, the agenda has continued to see many successes, and to achieve elements of political transformation large and small. This book explores how the supporting constituency of the agenda has 'made 1325 work'. Based on new interviews with representatives of diverse civil society organisations working on WPS, the book offers a novel intervention into WPS scholarship, which has thus far paid relatively little attention to the labours of civil society actors working on WPS, particularly on an individual level. The authors consider the motivations, pressures, and frustrations experienced by WPS civil society actors, as well as the goals and challenges.

This book is based on original research and will be of interest to scholars, policymakers, and practitioners working on WPS specifically, and those working in Political Science, International Relations, Development Studies, and on the global governance of peace and security. It will also be relevant for students in WPS-focused programmes and of peace and security studies more broadly.

Caitlin Hamilton is a Postdoctoral Research Fellow in Gender, Justice and Security at the University of Sydney, Australia. She is also the Managing Editor of the *Australian Journal of International Affairs*.

Anuradha Mundkur is an Adjunct Lecturer in the College of Humanities, Arts and Social Sciences at Flinders University, Australia. She is a member of the Australian Civil Society Coalition on Women, Peace and Security.

Laura J. Shepherd is Australian Research Council Future Fellow and Professor of International Relations at Sydney University, Australia. She is also a Visiting Senior Fellow at the LSE Centre for Women, Peace and Security in London, UK.

Routledge Studies in Gender and Global Politics
Series Editor: Laura J. Shepherd
University of Sydney, Australia

This series aims to publish books that work with, and through, feminist insights on global politics, and illuminate the ways in which gender functions not just as a marker of identity but also as a constitutive logic in global political practices. The series welcomes scholarship on any aspect of global political practices, broadly conceived, that pays attention to the ways in which gender is central to, (re)produced in, and is productive of, such practices.

There is growing recognition both within the academy and in global political institutions that gender matters in and to the practices of global politics. From the governance of peace and security, to the provision of funds for development initiatives, via transnational advocacy networks linked through strategic engagement with new forms of media, these processes have a gendered dimension that is made visible through empirically grounded and theoretically sophisticated feminist work.

Civil Society, Care Labour, and the Women, Peace and Security Agenda
Making 1325 Work

Caitlin Hamilton, Anuradha Mundkur and Laura J. Shepherd

Routledge
Taylor & Francis Group

LONDON AND NEW YORK

First published 2021
by Routledge
2 Park Square, Milton Park, Abingdon, Oxon OX14 4RN

and by Routledge
605 Third Avenue, New York, NY 10158

*Routledge is an imprint of the Taylor & Francis Group,
an informa business*

British Library Cataloguing-in-Publication Data
A catalogue record for this book is available from the
British Library

Library of Congress Cataloging-in-Publication Data
Names: Hamilton, Caitlin, author. | Mundkur, Anuradha,
    author. | Shepherd, Laura J., author.
Title: Civil society, care labour, and the women, peace and
    security agenda: making 1325 work/Caitlin Hamilton,
    Anuradha Mundkur and Laura J. Shepherd.
Description: Abingdon, Oxon; New York: Routledge, 2021. |
    Series: Routledge studies in gender and global politics |
    Includes bibliographical references and index.
Identifiers: LCCN 2020055439 (print) | LCCN 2020055440 (ebook) |
    ISBN 9780367642747 (hardback) | ISBN 9781003123750 (ebook)
Subjects: LCSH: Civil society. | Women and peace. | Women and human
    security. | Women–Violence against–Prevention–International
    cooperation. | United Nations. Security Council. Resolution 1325.
Classification: LCC JC337 .H35 2021 (print) | LCC JC337 (ebook) |
    DDC 362.83–dc23
LC record available at https://lccn.loc.gov/2020055439
LC ebook record available at https://lccn.loc.gov/2020055440

ISBN: 978-0-367-64274-7 (hbk)
ISBN: 978-0-367-64277-8 (pbk)
ISBN: 978-1-003-12375-0 (ebk)

Typeset in Times New Roman
by KnowledgeWorks Global Ltd.

This book is for the civil society actors who spoke with us in the course of this research, as well as their colleagues around the world. We are deeply appreciative of the work that you do in pursuit of peace. Thank you.

Contents

Acknowledgement

This research was funded by an Australian Research Council Discovery Project grant titled 'Rethinking the Women, Peace and Security Agenda in International, Transnational, and National Contexts' (DP160100212). We are grateful for the support and opportunities this grant afforded.

1 Care labour and social reproduction in the WPS agenda

The Women, Peace and Security (WPS) agenda has grown over the past two decades from the sustained feminist activism that brought matters of gender equality and the protection of women's rights during conflict and in conflict-affected settings to the attention of the international body charged with the maintenance of international peace and security: the United Nations Security Council. The Council debated these issues in October 2000 and adopted what became the first and foundational resolution in a sequence of resolutions adopted under the title of 'women and peace and security', thus forming the 'women and peace and security' agenda item, which is conventionally abbreviated to 'the WPS agenda'.

Over the course of two decades, and the adoption of ten resolutions,[1] the provisions and principles of the agenda have been well specified, and have cohered around four 'pillars' of activity: the participation of women at all stages and in all institutions of peace and security governance; the prevention of conflict, broadly, and more narrowly the prevention of sexual violence in conflict; the protection of women's rights in conflict and post-conflict reconstruction; and a commitment to gender-sensitive relief and recovery efforts. Formal and information political actors across the world, in national, regional, and international contexts, have taken up some or all of these pillars and have worked over the past two decades towards the full implementation of the WPS agenda, to secure the rights of women and girls in conflict, and to ensure that governance practices are enacted, and institutions operate, with due consideration for the gendered dynamics of peace and security.[2]

There are implementation plans to govern WPS work at the national level (known as 'national actions plans', or NAPs), at the regional level (including protocols and guidelines produced by the African Union, the European Union, and the Pacific Islands Forum), and within many international organisations, including a range of initiatives across the UN system, a portfolio of work under the auspices of the Organisation for Security and Co-operation in Europe (OSCE), and the formalisation, through the adoption of BI-Strategic Command Directive (BI-SCD) 40-1, of a commitment to WPS by the North Atlantic Treaty Organisation (NATO). The sheer volume of guidelines, protocols, and policies governing the implementation of the WPS agenda suggests that it has gained an unparalleled degree of traction for a normative agenda reliant on the UN Security Council for its formal policy articulations (see Kirby and Shepherd 2020 for a discussion of the complexity of the WPS agenda).[3] Unfortunately, many of these initiatives have not been entirely successful, with the shortcomings of implementation frequently being attributed primarily to limited political will and a lack of resources to support implementation (on funding in the WPS agenda see, for example, Koester et al. 2016; Esplen and O'Neill 2017; Skjelsbæk and Tryggestad 2019). 'Lack of financial resources coupled with insufficient prioritization and political commitment by decision-makers—from national governments or the UN alike—are commonly named the key factors for the disappointing implementation of the women, peace and security agenda' (Douglas and Mazzacurati 2017, p. 227).

There is no doubt that the shrinking allocation of resources to women's peace work more broadly, and to WPS specifically, in an era of increasing austerity worldwide affects the extent to which the goals and objectives of the WPS agenda can be realised. The agenda struggles in the absence of resources, and the political will to invest resources: 'true political will, and institutional commitment in the form of human and budgetary resources, have been in short supply' (Cohn 2017, pp. 4–5). There is no reason to believe that, over the next two decades, we will see much of an increase in that supply; particularly in the midst of the Covid-19 pandemic, when the majority of available resources are being redirected to primary service provision, economic stimulus and recovery packages, and public health campaigns, it is difficult to envisage that national governments or international organisations will spontaneously begin to provide adequate funding for women's peace work.

There have been some investment measures, such as the Global Acceleration Instrument (GAI), introduced in 2016 and rebranded the Women's Peace and Humanitarian Fund in 2019,[4] and allied initiatives such as the UN Peacebuilding Fund Gender Promotion Initiatives in 2011 and 2014, which compliments the use of a 'gender marker' to evaluate the extent to which activities supported by the Fund 'consider gender issues as part of the conflict analysis, priority setting, budget allocation, implementation, as well as in monitoring and evaluation' (UN Peacebuilding Fund, quoted in Shepherd 2017, p. 160). But on a global scale, these initiatives are a drop in the bucket. Moreover, only a few NAPs have a fully specified and dedicated budget to support implementation. 41% of all NAPs published in the period up to and including 2019 make no provision for budget whatsoever, and there is a distinct downward trend in the specification of budget in NAPs currently in place; '[o]ften, NAPs note that a budget is needed to undertake the WPS activities outlined, but there is no real specification of how much funding would be needed or from where this funding would come' (Hamilton, Naam and Shepherd 2020, p. 14). There is, therefore, no doubt that the WPS agenda receives insufficient resources to support full implementation. The question is: how has the WPS agenda enjoyed such success, achieved such traction, in the absence of adequate funding (and, in some cases, in the face of staunch political resistance to providing such funding)?

In this book, we argue that the work undertaken by civil society organisations, which represents a continuation of the mobilisation that germinated the WPS agenda, is integral to the agenda's (partial, qualified, sometimes limited) success. More specifically, we propose that the labour of civil society is a necessary component of what makes the WPS agenda possible – it is what makes resolution 1325 *work*. Civil society organisations were instrumental in laying the foundations of, and have since supported and pushed forward, the agenda (see, amongst others, Olsson and Gizelis 2013; Naraghi Anderlini 2019; Björkdahl and Mannergren Selimovic 2019). Civil society organisations drafted the first version of the text that became resolution 1325 and advocated for its adoption. Civil society organisations continue to monitor progress and push for greater implementation and accountability, as well as undertake research, advocacy and education, as we explore in the following chapter. These efforts are tremendous, but here we go beyond listing and lauding these contributions: we argue that the WPS work undertaken by civil society actors is a form of care labour that nourishes and sustains the agenda and, without it, the agenda could not, in fact, succeed.

This book grew out of a research project that involved many hours of conversations with people – mostly but not exclusively women – working on the WPS agenda as individuals or as part of formal civil society organisations. We interviewed representatives from 15 civil society organisations working on WPS based in North America, Europe, Asia, Africa, and Oceania. These are predominantly national organisations, rather than transnational (though, as discussed later on in the book, most are transnationally networked and many operate in coalition with other organisations and entities within and across national boundaries). The stories that our interview participants told were personal and honest. They included accounts of life journeys – of beginnings, and of family members and teachers who had offered them inspiration. They included challenges in specific workplaces, and communities, and they included personal frustrations, motivations, goals, and dreams. As such, and given our overriding commitment to maintaining the anonymity of those who were generous enough to share their stories with us, we have fully anonymised the data, with no identifier attached; this was a decision we came to in conversation with our research participants. This unusual measure stems from the concern that, taken together, a particular constellation of views, relationships, and struggles could, simply by virtue of how personal the stories were, create the possibility – however remote – of identification. As a manifestation of our commitment to ethical research, our participants were provided with a copy of their transcript to review, revise, and redact as they saw fit, and a copy of their quotes with a little context of how they would appear in this book, again with the opportunity to amend or remove them. Nonetheless, we would rather proceed with an abundance of caution given the precarity of the Agenda's funding model and the very real threats faced by some civil society actors working in WPS, and so comments from interviews are identified only as such.

We had intended originally to position this research as a parallel study to related projects investigating the stories told about the WPS agenda at the UN Headquarters in New York (Shepherd 2021) and the digital relationships between WPS organisations (Hamilton et al 2021). We expected that we would draw on these interviews to provide an account of the different ways in which the WPS agenda was unfolding and being implemented across the world, with each different elaboration representing an aspect of the WPS agenda such that the whole becomes visible through the aggregation of – and in the spaces between – its parts. No doubt this research would still be interesting to pursue, but as is the way of some research projects, the conversations we were having stubbornly refused to be bounded by our preconceived idea of what the research should be 'about'. Instead, the conversations we had with those working on, and for, the WPS agenda in their specific and situated contexts at a minimum had a palimpsest, a texture to the underside that was not about the substance of the WPS work these people were doing, but about how it *felt* to be doing this work: what motivated it; how they coped with the challenges; how they scratched for resources in an increasingly constrained funding environment; how they laboured, and laboured out of love and an abiding commitment to women's rights and gender equality.

It was this idea of labour, and love, to which our conversations kept returning. The people we spoke to often made time for us in their after-hours, went out of their way to connect us with colleagues or friends to continue the discussion, checked back in on us to see how the research was progressing. There was an inescapable feeling of care motivating their participation in the research. It began to feel impossible that we would write about the work that these people were doing and not the love, and the care; that it would somehow diminish or disregard the wholeness of the selves that they bring to their work. And so we began to try to make sense of the interviews we had conducted, the extensive, diverse, and wide-ranging conversations we had had with a group of advocates, activists, practitioners, and supporters of the WPS agenda through which there could be drawn these unexpected through-lines of commonality, of shared experience and connection even where no tangible or traceable link exists. These through-lines are the dimensions of care that we have used to structure this book.

To partner our thinking, we turned to literature from feminist political economy, where care and love have been theorised as part of the labour economy. This is a body of scholarship that has created space for understanding *reproduction* – in the sense of nurturing and sustaining human life – as an integral part of *production*: there can be no formal economic activity without the informal social relations of care and love that sustain the people who do the formal economic activity. In a series of turns between this theoretical literature and the transcribed interviews and conversations we had co-produced, the idea of WPS work as care labour began to take shape. Just as the formal economic production relies on – in fact cannot exist *without* – social reproduction, the success of the WPS agenda cannot be realised without the essential labour of the civil society organisations that sustain it. Simply put, this is the core argument of our book: the undervalued, under-appreciated, and often invisibilised labours of civil society, which we conceive of as nourishing and sustaining relations of care, are what make the WPS agenda work. The care labour of civil society is the very condition of the WPS agenda's success.

We develop this argument over the remaining five short chapters, before offering a brief conclusion. Chapter 2 follows and elaborates the concept of civil society, before providing an overview of the mobilisation of civil society in the form of civil society organisations in the work of the WPS agenda. We then explore literature on the activities of civil society organisations working on the WPS agenda, identifying three salient spheres of activity: advocacy, expert input, and implementation. Positioning civil society organisations as political actors lays for the foundation for offering a new conceptualisation of the work of civil society organisations within the WPS agenda. Chapter 3 completes the framework for analysis, as we bring to the foreground the intellectual labour undertaken by feminist global political economy scholars to take seriously and think through the various ways in which the politics, economics, and social dimensions of productive and reproductive economic activity are inextricably interlinked. In this chapter, we draw out the concepts from theories of social reproduction that enable an understanding of WPS labour as a form of care, and a resource that is a condition of the agenda's success.

Each of the subsequent chapters explores a dimension of care work that we propose is integral to making 1325 work: finding funding; dealing with despair; and maintaining the feminist commitment that is generative of so much WPS work. Chapter 4 tackles directly the persistent and chronic under-resourcing of the WPS agenda that remains one of the key challenges to its implementation. Civil society actors working in this space bear the brunt of this. Uncertainty around funding has led to the emergence of new and creative ways of resourcing work on the WPS agenda, and has also generated a significant volume of volunteer labour, which is 'invisibilised' and undervalued in conventional accounting of WPS resources. Perhaps deriving from the significance of civil society labour to the formation and development of the agenda, there is a habituated expectation that volunteer labour will and should sustain WPS activities. Funding for WPS work is rarely adequate, and almost never includes predictable and sustained core funding for the organisations that do the bulk of WPS programme delivery in many countries. For civil society organisations, the unfunded investment in constantly mobilising resources is the unpaid care work that allows them to achieve their vision and mandates.

Chapter 5 uses the concept of depletion, again taken from feminist political economy and theories of social reproduction, to draw out an analysis of the emotional impact of, and resilience required to, consistently deal with despair. The conversations we have had with civil society actors in the course of this research have drawn our attention to the extent of disillusionment that exists in relation to the WPS agenda. Sustaining hope that the transformative idea(l)s of the agenda will be realised motivates the continuing work and is therefore a form of emotional labour that the agenda relies upon. We draw out here the ways in which this labour manifests and can be made visible using the theoretical framework we develop in this work.

In the final substantive chapter, Chapter 6, we explore the work involved in bringing the agenda, and the actors involved in its implementation, back to its feminist foundations, which requires sustained advocacy and effort. The WPS agenda is (or at least could be) a radical political agenda that seeks to transform peace and security governance and bring an end to militarism and structural violence. There is labour that goes into maintaining a commitment to the feminist originating principles of the WPS agenda. Civil society organisations frequently espouse a commitment to holistic approaches to peace and to the prevention of conflict – but are concerned that these elements are being lost in 1325 work.

Chapter 7 offers a brief conclusion to the strands of argument we develop throughout the book and reflects on some of the limitations of the work we present in this book. We also reflect on the 'power and danger', to use Dianne Otto's words (2010), of theorising women's peace work as care labour, acknowledging that drawing on theories of social reproduction risks naturalising the work that civil society organisations do in service of the WPS agenda, in the same way that care labour in the domestic realm is still persistently presumed to be 'natural' and is therefore consistently unappreciated and underfunded. We conclude that bringing theoretical work on social reproduction, and in particular the attendant concept of *depletion* through social reproduction (Rai, Hoskyns and Thomas 2014, p. 88; we elaborate on this concept in Chapters 3 and 5 in particular), demands that the care labour of civil society is counted and accounted for, recognised as an exhaustible resource and a condition of the agenda's success; we follow in the footsteps of feminist political economists here in arguing that valuing such labour 'becomes a communication tool by translating unpaid work into a language governments understand: money' (Hoskyns and Rai 2007, p. 302).

This is not a particularly weighty tome in any sense: we offer here a relatively brief account of a limited project involving a quite small group of people working in a niche area of women's rights and peace activism, and we draw on established theories of social reproduction to make sense of the information that was shared with us by our research participants. Thus, we are not offering grand innovations here; rather, by combining the insights of feminist political economy with the stories shared with us by those doing WPS work, we offer a new vocabulary with which to describe and debate the political terrain of the WPS agenda. Crucially, although this book is positioned as an 'academic' text (in that we anticipate that our primary readership is likely to be researchers and students and that we seek to contribute in a modest way to academic debates), it is also a book that we hope will resonate with the practitioner and advocacy communities making 1325 work. In these pages, we do our best to present honestly and accurately the accounts of WPS work shared with us by those who keep the agenda alive, and we recognise their labour – the love and care they extend to the agenda in all its diversity – as an essential part of what makes 1325 work.

Notes

1. The resolutions, with year of adoption, are UNSCR 1325 (2000), UNSCR 1820 (2008), UNSCR 1888 (2009), UNSCR 1889 (2009), UNSCR 1960 (2010), UNSCR 2106 (2013), UNSCR 2122 (2013), UNSCR 2242 (2015), UNSCR 2467 (2019), and UNSCR 2493 (2019).
2. The scholarly literature on the WPS agenda has proliferated enormously over the past two decades. It is obviously impossible to survey the extent of this literature in an endnote, but excellent overviews of the histories of the agenda and its contested development are provided by, among others: Hill, Aboitiz, and Poehlman-Doumbouya (2003); Cohn, Kinsella and Gibbings (2004); Naraghi Anderlini (2007); and cook (2009). More recent efforts to survey the agenda and the field of scholarship that has grown in parallel may also be useful for the unfamiliar reader, including: Hans and Rajagopalan (2016); Manchanda (2017); Davies and True (2019); and Basu, Kirby, and Shepherd (2020).
3. All Security Council resolutions are binding on UN member states but the WPS resolutions are not adopted under Chapter 7 of the UN Charter, which means that they have a normative rather than legal status (see: Otto 2010; Heathcote 2011, 2012, 2018; Charlesworth and Chinkin 2013).
4. At the time of writing, only 11 member states have invested in the Global Acceleration Instrument: Australia, Austria, Canada, Ireland, Japan, Liechtenstein, Lithuania, the Netherlands, Norway, Spain, and the United Kingdom.

2 Civil society and the WPS agenda

Multiple accounts of the Women, Peace and Security (WPS) agenda begin with stories of the civil society advocacy surrounding the adoption of UNSCR 1325 in 2000, framing which is of critical importance in shaping what the agenda could and would become in the intervening twenty years (see, among many others: Porter 2003; El-Bushra 2007; Shepherd 2008; Naraghi Anderlini 2019; Björkdahl and Mannergren Selimovic 2019). The impact on the agenda of the women's civil society organisations that lobbied for the adoption of the foundational resolution is a touchstone of political activism around the agenda and has had a significant effect on the development of the agenda over the past two decades. In particular, the way that women's civil society organisations are acknowledged as both influential and invested in the agenda has sustained the involvement of those organisations in both ritualised celebrations of the agenda (for example, in the annual Open Debates at the Security Council on the theme) and in implementation efforts. Diverse civil society actors remain active in WPS practice and the inclusion of civil society organisations in the formulation and implementation of WPS National Action Plans is acknowledged as one of the key indicators of a high-impact plan (Jonjić-Beitter, Stadler, and Tietgen 2020). In this chapter, we explore the mobilisation of civil society in the form of civil society organisations working on and with the WPS agenda.[1] We engage with literature on the activities of civil society organisations working on the WPS agenda, identifying three salient themes: representation, diversity, and agency. Positioning civil society organisations as political actors lays for the foundation for analysing the work of civil society organisations within the WPS agenda.

In modern political theory, the concept of civil society was juxtaposed with the 'state of nature', in which people enjoy neither the freedom afforded by, nor the protections of, formal government. *Societas civilis*, in this view, is broadly synonymous with subjection to the rule of law and the civilisation of society under democratic rule (Kumar 1993; Black 2001; Keane 2010). Our view of civil society is one that engages with the *'articulation* and *negotiation* of political interests within society' with the outcome of effecting positive change (Spurk 2010, p. 8; emphasis in original), while remaining in balance with government because CSOs lack the regulatory and geostrategic power of states. John Keane has proposed that 'civil society should become a permanent thorn in the side of political power' (Keane 1989, p. 15), but in such a way as the state and civil society are mutually reinforcing progressive initiatives and alternative visions of social organisation. This conceptualisation of civil society and its function vis-à-vis social progress leaves unanswered questions about *why* civil society is such a valuable sphere of activity. A well-thought-through account of the benefits of a vibrant and engaged civil society requires that we sketch out the positive qualities or characteristics of civil society participation in governance, lest we present an analysis that romanticises or obscures rather than clarifies the contributions made by civil society organisations in relation to WPS governance.

Debates about the inclusion of civil society in WPS governance in particular owe an intellectual debt to debate about civil society as a development actor, which is not unrelated to Keane's discussion of democratisation. While there are numerous 'bottom-up' explanations for the proliferation of civil society actors, including increased investment in democratic governance and increased connectivity across national boundaries (Reimann 2006, pp. 45–46), there are important 'top-down' factors at play also. In the context of societal transformation, particularly transformation led by global development organisations in the 1980s and 1990s, 'a vibrant civil society was considered an important pillar for establishing democracy, and support for it became an obvious aim of democratization' (Schmidt, cited in Spurk 2010, p. 16). In this period, many governance incentives engendered the growth and increased mobilisation of non-governmental organisations and other civil society actors; 'the expansion of institutions of global governance over time ... produced new international political opportunities for NGOs that have spurred their growth' (Reimann 2006, p. 46). The growth of the 'third sector' – neither government nor private business – has been remarkable in many parts of the world across the spheres of development, humanitarian work, peacebuilding, and social welfare. The significance of, and value in, fostering an engaged civil society in the context of development carries over to, and inform assessments of, the significance and worth of civil society engagement with WPS principles and practices.

Civil society engagement with WPS has tended to be through the mobilisation of civil society actors through coalitions and in formal civil society organisations. The Women and Armed Conflict Caucus, for example, was instrumental in laying out the foundations for advocacy actions that created space for resolution 1325. In March of 2000, while Bangladesh held the Presidency of the Council, the Women and Armed Conflict Caucus made a strong statement to the Commission on the Status of Women (CSW) regarding 'obstacles to implementing the chapter of the Beijing Platform for Action ... devoted to women and armed conflict' (Hill, Aboitiz and Poehlman-Doumbouya 2003, p. 1256). Soon after, in May of the same year, the Non-Governmental Organisation Working Group on Women, Peace and Security (NGO WG on WPS) was formed 'to pursue two recommendations – to encourage women's participation in peace agreements and to push for the convening of a special session of the Security Council', which would eventually lead to the adoption of UNSCR 1325 (Hill, Aboitiz and Poehlman-Doumbouya 2003, p. 1258). Thus, as noted earlier, civil society organisations are frequently credited with providing the impetus for the consolidation of the range of issues affecting women in conflict, with the crystallisation of these issues into a UN Security Council resolution and, later, extending this resolution to form an agenda.

In the two decades since the adoption of resolution 1325, civil society organisations have played an active role in the further development and implementation of the WPS agenda. Their engagement with the WPS agenda typically falls into three broad categories of activity: advocacy (primarily but not exclusively related to national and international governance institutions), expert input (where representatives of civil society organisations or unaffiliated individuals provide advice on matters related to the WPS agenda), and implementation (where civil society organisations are involved in formal or informal implementation activities).

Resolution 1325 was adopted as a result of concerted advocacy on the part of women's civil society organisations and representatives. Thus, advocacy is perhaps the most well-established sphere of activity in which civil society organisations working on the WPS agenda are involved. This role has been sustained in the intervening years, with advocacy in diverse national and international contexts contributing to the development of the agenda. The NGO Working Group on WPS, formed in 2000, is still involved in advocacy at UN Headquarters and with the diplomatic missions of UN member states in New York, particularly around the Security Council but extending to other UN entities as needed. The NGO Working Group represents 18 separate member organisations in a consensus-based coalition; the work of the group includes the development of advocacy papers underpinned by independent monitoring and analysis of the implementation of the WPS agenda across the UN system and by member states in their domestic politics. Within the domestic political context of UN member states, there are many other coalitions and organisations formed to advocate for the full implementation of the WPS agenda in their national contexts, which sometimes – though not always – similarly function to represent the interests of smaller national organisations (or national branches of international non-governmental organisations) along with the expertise of individuals.[2]

Advocacy is thus one of the established ways in which civil society (including individuals, non-governmental organisations, coalitions, and networks) works on and with the WPS agenda. Advocacy initiatives and efforts represent a defined space in which civil society organisations (and sometimes individuals) are permitted – even encouraged – to engage with the WPS agenda, though the politics of advocacy around the WPS agenda are not necessarily unproblematic. Scholars have identified, for example, the racialised and disempowering dynamics of certain formats of advocacy particularly at UN Headquarters. When allowed to participate in discussions at UN Headquarters, the agency of civil society actors – particularly but not exclusively women from conflict-affected settings – is constrained; they are expected to communicate and act in specific ways that align with pre-existing ideas about subjectivity, agency, and empowerment.[3]

Related to, though separate from, advocacy, another mode of engagement by civil society organisations with the WPS agenda is in the provision of expert input on WPS-related issues. Women from conflict-affected settings are brought to brief the UN Security Council each year at the Open Debate because their experience matters; they are assumed to have particularly pertinent insights into WPS-related matters as a result of their lived experience in conflict. Additionally, through the formation of the Informal Expert Group on WPS in 2016, civil society organisations have another avenue for input: prior to each meeting 'UN-Women consults with the relevant United Nations entities at Headquarters and in the field, and civil society, to prepare the background reading and key recommendations' (S/2016/1106, p. 5).

Recognising women's expertise in the field of peace and security is an important component of the WPS project. Put simply, women and women's CSOs have a right to participate in WPS governance because they have expertise that will enable or facilitate the achievements of the goals and objectives under discussion. In a broader sense, this is in keeping with analysis of civil society participation that identifies an epistemic rationale for the inclusion of CSOs in decision-making and policy formulation. If we accept that, '[i]n order to have good rules, we should bring the experiences, reasons, and perspectives that policy makers and government-appointed experts would not otherwise consider in to the decision-making process' (Steffek and Ferretti 2009, pp. 40–41), then the input of civil society in such deliberations is legitimised through the ascription of the subject-position of 'expert' to the civil society participant simultaneously as the participation of civil society is justified on the basis of the participant's expertise: the two concepts go hand-in-hand and are mutually reinforcing.

Civil society organisations' involvement in the WPS agenda also takes the form of implementation efforts. Many CSOs deliver WPS and WPS-related programmes; some receive government funding to deliver WPS programmes and undertake WPS-related humanitarian work, while others rely on philanthropy and street-level fundraising. In Nigeria, for example, women-led civil society organisations engage in gender-responsive initiatives to counter violent extremism, undertaking a range of activities including 'provision of relief materials, protest marches, press conferences, advocacy visits to major stakeholders, socio-economic services, rehabilitation of critical infrastructure and participation in early warning workshops' (Nwangwu and Ezeibe 2019, p. 177). Similarly, in Afghanistan, women's CSOs 'have played an instrumental role so far in outreach and awareness raising, training and capacity building, and facilitating engagement between women and other important actors at the community level' in efforts to counter extremism (Safi 2016, p. 126). In this way, civil society organisations are frequently 'service providers', funded directly to undertake specific functions within a defined programme of activity, or working informally within their communities.

Across the domains of advocacy, expert input to WPS-related discussions, and implementation, civil society organisations are thus intrinsic to the continued development and maintenance of the WPS agenda. Despite these widespread and varied activities, consistent and reliable funding for civil society organisations involved in WPS work remains rare. The majority of WPS funding received by CSOs in the global majority is donor-driven, consisting of direct bilateral funding to governments from donors, supplemented by international and multinational organisations, and a handful of direct grants (Barrow 2009; Miller, Pournik and Swaine 2014, p. 9). Research on the implementation of the WPS agenda consistently remarks on the severe under-resourcing of WPS activities and a downward trend in

WPS funding (Coomaraswamy et al. 2015; Khan 2017; Skjelsbæk and Tryggestad 2019, p. 521), despite the significant role that CSOs have in WPS-related activities.

The persistent under-funding of WPS civil society organisations motivates a reconsideration of what these organisations are doing and why. As outlined above, their work is intrinsic to the success of the WPS agenda, but they are rarely remunerated for the work that they do, and individuals within, and allied with, these organisations frequently volunteer their labour in order to achieve specific objectives. Academic research and institutional evaluations alike suggest that many dimensions of the WPS agenda are under-budgeted or under-resourced. Where state governments are not providing sufficient budget specification, or resources, to manifest commitment to the implementation of the WPS agenda, this can be understood in terms of a lack of support, or a lack of political will. The continued investment of civil society labour despite the lack of material support is less easy to explain. Moreover, it appears that this work is a condition of the agenda's continuation. If this labour is not motivated by a transactional logic – resources exchanged for expertise or services – then it is reasonable to explore alternative ways to think about this kind of work, what motivates it, and what functions it has in the maintenance and development of the WPS agenda. Thus, in the following chapter, we turn to the concepts of social reproduction and care labour developed in feminist political economy to make sense of the efforts of civil society that seem to make 1325 work.

Notes

1. This section draws on previously published work of two of the authors (Mundkur and Shepherd 2018).
2. Examples include Gender Action for Peace and Security (GAPS) UK, the Australian Civil Society Coalition on Women, Peace and Security, and the Women, Peace and Security Network Canada.
3. Shweta Singh (2017) refers to this as 'controlled agency' in her analysis of WPS civil society activity in Sri Lanka.

3 Care labour as a condition of the agenda's success

Civil society organisations, and less formal social movements, alongside and in collaboration with committed individual activists and advocates, were essential to the drafting and eventual adoption of UN Security Council resolution 1325, the cornerstone of the Women, Peace and Security agenda. As Cynthia Cockburn notes, 'It may well be the only Security Council resolution for which the groundwork, the diplomacy and lobbying, the drafting and redrafting, was almost entirely the work of civil society, of non-governmental organisations. Certainly, it was the first in which the actors were almost all women' (Cockburn 2007, p. 141). As the agenda has continued to develop, and the range of activities associated with the WPS agenda has continued to expand, it is widely recognised that civil society actors are leaders in both advocacy and lobbying for greater recognition of the WPS agenda and in drafting resolutions, policies, and action plans for its effective implementation.

Many studies also draw attention to the woefully inadequate funding provided to enable civil society participation, which is a near-universal concern. In other related work, for example, Mundkur and Shepherd conclude their analysis by arguing forcefully that 'taking seriously—and facilitating properly, *including through funding* and opportunities for direct consultation—women's civil society participation in WPS governance ... is essential for the agenda's continued resonance, legitimacy, and efficacy in world politics' (2018, p. 103, emphasis added). As discussed in Chapter 1, the shortcomings and failures of the WPS agenda more broadly are often attributed to a material lack of resources committed to ensuring sustainable success. Indeed, given the 'short supply' of 'human and budgetary resources' committed to the WPS agenda across the world (Cohn 2017, pp. 4–5), it is remarkable that the agenda has enjoyed the successes that it has. This point is central to the argument that we develop throughout this book, and it is the linchpin of the theoretical framework we develop in this chapter, because we propose that the successes of the WPS agenda are attributable in large part to the extensive engagement of civil society in unpaid, unrecognised, and under-theorised labour in the realm of WPS work.[1]

Women's civil society organisations and individual actors care deeply about the agenda. This is evident in narratives from women peacebuilders and women's human rights defenders when they discuss their feelings about the foundational resolution and the agenda more broadly. Sanam Naraghi Anderlini, for example, who was closely involved with the adoption of resolution 1325 and the development of the agenda in those early years, reports in her book about women's peacebuilding activities, '[u]pon the first anniversary [of the passage of UNSCR 1325], in 2001, the Council members expressed surprise. "Other resolutions don't have anniversaries", they said, to which the NGOs replied, "Other resolutions don't have a global constituency"' (Naraghi Anderlini 2007, p. 7). Naraghi Anderlini here draws our attention to a 'global constituency' of care committed to the success of the agenda. Similarly, Mavic Cabrera-Balleza, co-founder and international coordinator of the Global Network of Women Peacebuilders, affirms the affective dimension of civil society engagement, using language of physical proximity, even intimacy, when she comments: 'I still recall one GNWP member from the conflict-affected Mount Elgon district in Kenya who said to me: "The first time I read Resolution 1325, *I held it close to my chest.* This is ours; this belongs to us"' (Cabrera-Balleza 2011, emphasis added). It is certainly unusual to see a Security Council resolution described as something a person would hold close, and engage in an affectionate or intimate way. This points to the care that is invested in the agenda by its advocates and proponents, which has (at least) two dimensions: the sense of care and commitment to the issues that motivated the agenda; and the continuing relations of care that nurture and sustain it. These considerations highlight the need to critically interrogate care and its practice as a condition of success in the realm of the WPS agenda.

To explore the political expression and function of care, we turn to feminist scholarship on the global political economy, which has brought to the surface for analytical scrutiny many invisible or deeply naturalised processes and dynamics that are in fact, when made visible, highly contingent and political – and leveraged in service of political ends.[2] Early feminist global political economy work (including, for example Boserup 1970; Benería 1979; Benería and Sen 1981) was profoundly influential in the development of new ways to evaluate economic activity that took seriously what gender-unaware work on the global political economy ignored: the gendered assumptions embedded in conventional and formal calculations and also the gendered dynamics of economic activity, which associated certain forms of work and behaviour with bodies coded masculine and other forms of work and behaviour with their feminine/feminised counterparts. As Penny Griffin explains 'analysing gender as a governing code exposes the stories, assumptions and practices that we attach to human bodies and makes visible the gendered practices that conventional IPE [international political economy] has sought to conceal' (Griffin 2010, p. 96). Among the transformative insights developed by these feminist scholars was the articulation of the gendered processes of reproduction that were essential to the perpetuation of economic production. These scholars took seriously, and argued with persuasive clarity, for the need to integrate into calculations of economic activity the work undertaken beyond the formal economic sector that makes productive economic activity possible. The concept of 'social reproduction' captures this dimension of labour, identifying 'not only biological reproduction but also the "social provisioning" needed to maintain individuals, groups and communities and underpin economic and other activity' (Hoskyns 2008, p. 111).

We find the conceptualisation of social reproduction offered by Catherine Hoskyns and Shirin Rai (2007) compelling, as it presents not only a range of social processes that underpin formal economic activity but also captures the intangible dimensions of relational practices that are frequently absent from economistic discussions of value.[3] Their conceptualisation is worth quoting at length:

> [S]ocial reproduction can be taken to include the following: biological reproduction; unpaid production in the home (both goods and services); social provisioning (by this we mean voluntary work directed at meeting needs in the community); the reproduction of culture and ideology; and the provision of sexual, emotional and affective services (such as are required to maintain family and intimate relationships). These are all elements contributed to the economy and society in general by the household and the community. They are mainly contributed by women, regardless of their position in society and the resources they can muster to manage the pressures and rewards associated with social reproduction.
>
> (Hoskyns and Rai 2007, p. 300)

This is an expansive definition and one which incorporates material and non-material factors that are intrinsic to the maintenance of formal economic activity. It therefore extends the original feminist insight that biological reproductive activity is necessary for the creation of bodies to provide labour and produce goods and services. The critical point that we wish to foreground here is the intellectual labour undertaken by feminist GPE scholars to take seriously and think through the various ways in which the politics, economics, and social dimensions of productive and reproductive economic activity are inextricably interlinked.

Focussing on reproductive labour provides us with a vocabulary with which to elaborate on the concept of care as it is imbricated with political-economic activity. As noted above, care has been theoretically engaged as a component of social reproduction, drawing on scholarship beyond feminist global political economy.[4] Care, broadly conceived as a consideration of, and commitment to, the well-being of others, is inherently relational, and essential to social reproduction, if the latter is seen to capture both 'the reproduction of people as physical beings and the reproduction of social identities within given social and cultural contexts' (Bjeren 1997, cited in Kofman 2012, p. 144). 'This definition is able to accommodate an incredibly wide range of activities, ranging from highly intimate social, health and sexual care services to less intimate ones such as cooking, cleaning, ironing and general maintenance work' (Yeates 2004, p. 371). Thus, care is essential not only to individual well-being but also to the well-being of societies; through this analytical lens, relations of care – and social reproduction – are rendered visible and able to be integrated into evaluations of economic value and activity.

There are two dimensions of care that we find particularly resonant and useful as we elaborate our theorisation of care as underpinning the success of the WPS agenda. First, there is the extent to which the association of care with labour, especially when 'care labour' is analysed with a concern for the operation of gendered power, draws attention to the burden placed upon individuals – predominantly women – by the diminution or cessation of state-supported or state-enacted caring activities. One of the primary and most significant insights from feminist political economists about the care economy is its presumed infinite capacity to absorb additional workload that is unrewarded by the formal economic sector and the infinite flexibility – as well as 'natural' propensity/skill – of women to take on this work (Bakker 2007, p. 546). A classic example is the expectation that women will 'pick up the slack' by engaging in more childcare, more care of elders, and more relational caregiving where state childcare provision, elder care facilities, and mental health care provision are defunded. Recognising the tremendous burden that this additional, often invisible, labour represents, feminist political economists have developed the concept of 'depletion through social reproduction', which affects individuals and households 'when there is a critical gap between the outflows – domestic, affective and reproductive – and the inflows that sustain their health and well-being' (Rai, Hoskyns and Thomas 2014, p. 86; for elaboration of the concept of depletion through social reproduction, see also Rai, True and Tanyag 2019). The construction of political-economic systems that depend upon the 'voluntary' labour of individuals – again, mostly women – for their continued success, and which do not factor ways to ensure that the individuals providing care are not themselves exhausted by these interactions, is both exploitative and extractive *by design*.[5] We return to this concept in Chapter 5.

The second aspect of care that we find particularly useful to think with is the elaboration of care within the concept of 'global care chains' (Hochschild 2000; Yeates 2004, 2009; Kofman 2012). Developed in feminist scholarship on migration practices, the concept of global care chains captures 'transnational care services and the international division of reproductive labour as integral features of the contemporary international economy' (Yeates 2004, p. 370). In an increasingly globalised and interconnected world, care labour is not spatially or even physically contained: grandparents read stories to children half a world away using digital videoconferencing technologies, while people travel far beyond their countries of origin to provide care for other people's children or elders of other families. The dis-location of care and its borderless, limitless *need* is a central aspect of political-economic activity in late modernity. It is not unrelated to the changing patterns of governance under neoliberalism, with its attendant demands of flexibilisation and 'agility' in responding to the 'needs' of the market, which in turn enhance efficiency: 'neo-liberalism indicted the welfare state for being wasteful, paternalistic, and ineffective, recommending instead, the freeing up of old markets and the creation of new ones' (Brodie 2003, p. 60). One of these new markets is the commodification of (self-)care on the one hand – the ability to quantify the value of well-being and market this ephemeral condition to sell juice cleanses and yoga mats – and, on the other hand, the interpellation of individuals, many of whom are structurally disadvantaged in hierarchies of race and gender (see Peterson 2002), into circuits of care that are still not afforded value within conventional calculations of productivity. 'Women's reproductive labor is bracketed out as having no market value or, at best, existing as an externality' (Brodie 2003, p. 62). The concept of 'chains' of care helps us make sense of the relations that connect the various civil society actors we engaged in our research, and we return to this concept in Chapter 6.

This exploration of care and the broader concept of social reproduction clearly have great utility for the exploration of formal and informal economic practices. The argument that we present here is that these concepts have applicability beyond the context within which they were developed, and can be used to think in the realm of peace work as well as economics. Sparked by the many conversations we were having (and continue to have) in our academic research, activism, and advocacy related to the WPS agenda, in which our interlocutors frequently and near-universally use language resonant of social reproduction, we seek to bring in the concept of care to our thinking about what makes the WPS agenda work. Participants in our research have discussed with us their commitment to nurturing and maintaining the agenda, to securing the resources necessary to ensure its continued feasibility, to building the relational connections that will sustain it: this is the language of care labour, applied not to the reproduction of human life and society but to a policy agenda.

We are not the first to expand the concept of care beyond its original context. Shirin Rai, Jacqui True, and Maria Tanyag extend Rai's earlier work on depletion through social reproduction to propose that 'the recognition and redistribution of care should be an integral part of conflict response and peacebuilding. At present, however, unpaid care labor is hardly recognized or supported by state and international actors in postconflict reconstruction' (2019, p. 562). Rai, True, and Tanyag examine the care labour activities undertaken by women in post-conflict settings and argue persuasively that household care economies should be properly evaluated and valued in accounting for post-conflict reconstruction (2019, p. 563). Similarly, Tiina Vaittinen and her co-authors approach peacebuilding through the lens of care, to mount a compelling case for recognising the extent to which, in their three case studies, 'relations of care emerge as a dynamic for processes of trust-building, community-building, and peaceful transformation' (Vaittinen et al. 2019, p. 207). There is an implicit parallel in the political activities that these authors describe between the care labour undertaken by women in Iceland after the 2007/2008 global financial crisis and the labour of civil society actors related to the WPS agenda. In an effort to engage and influence government policy,

Reykjavík city councillor Sóley Tómasdóttir created a Facebook group, called 'the women's emergency government' (*Neyðarstjórn kvenna*), and issued a manifesto for a women's collective that would promote the reconstruction of a community based on humane values, emphasizing respect for the individual, community, life, nature and the environment.

(Vaittinen et al. 2019, p. 205)

While Vaittinen et al. explore these caring relationships in an analysis of peacebuilding and the aftermath of crisis, we argue that such efforts occur in varied and disparate contexts during 'peacetime' and during and 'after' conflict such that this type of organising can be conceived of as care labour in the policy sphere in 'peacetime' as well as in relation to crisis and post-conflict reconstruction.

The essence of our theoretical claim here is that, just as the formal economy relies on social reproduction and specifically the care labour undertaken mostly by women and others positioned precariously within structures of power, so too does the success of the WPS agenda as a sphere of political activity rely on reproductive and care labour undertaken by those who are often marginalised and devalued even as they are overworked. Thus, the agenda's success *is dependent on* ('voluntary', un[der]funded, un[der]valued) care and reproductive activity just as economic success relies on the continued practices of social reproduction highlighted by feminist political economics over the last five decades. The types of care labour undertaken by political actors – mostly civil society actors, who are both feminised and who are empirically mostly women in the realm of WPS activity – are varied, but map on to the care labour undertaken in the economic realm by that sphere's precariat. While economically, care labour reproduces bodies as resources for capital, in policy, care labour reproduces financial resource, by advocating for or securing funding for WPS-related programs and activities. Care labour also reproduces the policy architecture itself, by contributing (often unpaid) expertise and knowledge to the policymaking institutions. Similarly, care labour in policy is channelled into the development of networks and relationships that contribute to the spread of norms and the mobilisation of constellations of meaning to provide a semblance of fixity in/to WPS ideas, such as 'prevention' or 'participation'. Finally, care labour is evident in the work of civil society actors seeking to 'keep the dream of 1325 alive'. The ideological commitment to the principles of 1325 is not translated and transmitted across borders and through time by policy documents: these are brought to life by the agenda's keepers, and the unrecognised reproductive labour they invest. As feminist political economists have recently begun to explore the affective domain of care labour, we argue that the care labour undertaken by civil society actors in relation to the WPS agenda is critically important to the agenda's continuation and success.

Thus, we identify three dimensions of reproductive labour, which we elaborate on throughout the remainder of this book. Each of the subsequent chapters explores a dimension of care work that we propose is integral to making 1325 work: (1) finding funding; (2) dealing with despair; and (3) maintaining the feminist commitment that is generative of so much WPS work. These efforts, conceived of as demonstrations of care and dimensions of the reproductive labour undertaken by civil society organisations, activists, and advocates for women's rights, are essential to the success of the WPS agenda. Quite simply, we could not make 1325 work without this labour, and the converse is also true: most governance structures that support activity related to the WPS agenda rely on the provision of such labour (which is woefully undervalued and often completely unrewarded) and thus construct 1325 work as undervalued and unrewarded reproductive labour. Civil society makes 1325 work, but 1325 also makes a lot of unpaid, unrecognised, and unvalued work for civil society.

Notes

1. We are grateful to Penny Griffin, who provided insightful comments and feedback on an early draft of this chapter. Mistakes and omissions, of course, remain our own.
2. Such processes and dynamics include care, of course, and also, for example, emotional labour and affective labour; see Sauer and Penz (2017).
3. Relatedly, see also V. Spike Peterson's work on the 'virtual economy' (Peterson 2002, 2003).
4. Notably, feminist ethics and moral philosophy; see the discussion in Vaittinen et al. (2019).
5. Kate Bedford (2008, p. 86) calls this 'an exhaustion solution' to the policy problem of notionally affording value to social reproduction while simultaneously recognising in practice only the economic value of productive labour.

4 Funding

The WPS agenda is chronically under-resourced. That was the key message that came through from everyone that we spoke to in the course of this research. In the absence of consistent, reliable funding, civil society organisations are forced to navigate between two equally unsatisfactory imperatives: the need to devote time and energy to finding funding, on the one hand, to support those activities which absolutely require investment; and the need to take on significant amounts of unpaid work, on the other hand, to keep on with WPS work in the absence of material support. The limited funding that does exist – which tends to come from states, international non-government organisations (INGOs), private/philanthropic donors, and fundraising – tends to be unpredictable, insufficient and often cobbled together from multiple sources. The recipients, requirements, kinds of funding and dynamics of these funding streams vary significantly (see, for example, Pinter 2001).

Much of what is funded is in the form of project-based contractual arrangements with local organisations, who then deliver the work. As two of our research participants explained:

> The discussions are ongoing, and it is very frustrating. I think there is a political will, but finding that right funding source where you fit the criteria – you sort of say at one point 'if we're this important to you, you should be able to find a way to fund us'. Then you get the response 'we're working on it'. We did receive some support… for consultations pre-NAP, where the government funded a two-day workshop, but [it was] minor and project specific.

> The [redacted] government is a donor, but then also, yes, it is over-whelmingly, if not exclusively for project-based mandates and

funding. But because we're also affiliated with [redacted], there are also funding contributions [from other sources]... So, I think the money comes in from a couple of different places, but it's almost overwhelmingly project-based.

Project-based funding poses a set of problems and politics. First, it makes medium- to long-term planning very difficult for civil society, who do not know what funding, if any, will exist to undertake future activities or programs. As one interviewee explained:

> This year, at the moment, we are still finalising the final report; we also keep going, discussing, meetings, workshops, seminars provided by [funders], and also thinking of how can we keep monitoring Women, Peace and Security, and we do not know yet, maybe another opportunity, finding another financial support. Maybe we can continue, but we don't know yet.

Second, it often fails to provide for the mundane but necessary general expenditure involved in running a CSO – for printer paper and postage, for example, or rent for workspaces. In some cases, civil society actors have effectively been *paying* to do their work:

> We asked members to start paying a membership fee... [I]t's a start of a little bit of a budget to pay for coffee and book rooms and things like that. Up until now, people were paying out of their own pocket.

The perverse performance measures of overhead cost ratios are starving small, grassroots, often women-led CSOs like those implementing the WPS agenda. Overhead costs fund the care and maintenance of organisations. CSOs with lower overhead cost ratios (all expenses that are not related to programs, and therefore, do not directly create impact, relative to the budget) are favoured by donors – the logic being that in such cases, more money is spent delivering project outcomes (Burkart, Wakolbinger, and Toyasaki 2018). As a result, small, grassroots CSOs often find themselves competing with large INGOs, which are more easily able to absorb decreasing the ratio of overheads to gain a competitive advantage in donor markets. Lecy and Searing (2015) call this the 'non-profit starvation cycle' as it results in increasing the pressure on organisations to keep reducing costs in a race to the bottom.

Civil society organisations therefore navigate difficult terrain when it comes to seeking and allocating funds; the organisations must secure both adequate resourcing for existing programs and a consistent flow of resources to enable the organisation to operate effectively into the future. Much of the success in sustaining future inflow of resources depends on (and is indeed premised on) the building, maintaining and nurturing of relationships with funders or investing in fundraising – in other words, the unpaid care work involved implementing and advancing the WPS agenda. This effort represents an added time burden on staff in small CSOs, who are often doing resource mobilisation work in addition to their primary roles. A consequence of this resource-intensive yet unpaid care work (in terms of cost and time) is that small CSOs end up having to make choices with respect to investing in sustainability over other resource-intensive work like advocacy, influence and holding governments to account. The end result is a shrinking civic space.

Third, the effective outsourcing of the grunt work in project-based funding results in CSOs being treated 'as contractors rather than change makers and innovators' (Esplen 2013, p. 8). Scott Freeman and Mark Schuller (2020) argue that 'the project has become the dominant form of disbursing aid' resulting in an increasing commodification of development where 'exchange value can take precedence over services provided' (p. 1). This, in turn, shifts the focus from outcome and impact to seeking visibility through documentation. What makes this problematic, Freeman and Schuller argue, is that the focus on documentation reduces communities and people to numbers – number of people reached or trained or who attended meeting or hours worked. Erica Caple James (2010) calls into account practices that reduce people to reports and trauma portfolios, which organisations can use for institutional gain. Essentially this need to be made visible through documentation, in order to win other project funding, creates performative subjectivities which is a far cry from the transformative potential of the WPS agenda (see, for example, Freeman and Schuller 2020, writing about Haiti tent camps). In other words, 'as projects are commodified they mask the activities and labour that contribute to the project documents and obfuscate the very political processes of commodity production' (Freeman and Schuller, 2020, p. 9). We agree with Freeman and Schuller that in order to unpack the labour, especially the unpaid labour, that goes into producing visibility we need to ask 'what sort of labour is involved in producing projects? If the production of project documents is ultimately at the heart of the political economy of aid, who gains from such economies, and who stands to lose?' (p. 8).

Fourth, project-based funding means that a smaller group of funders have a disproportionate say in what matters to the agenda, the issues that should be researched, and the kinds of activities that should be undertaken. This is sometimes done very intentionally and consciously – for example, the way in which the United States placed conditions on funding relating to reproductive services. In some cases, though, it simply represents a discord between an understanding of priorities in the area of policy compared to the on the ground lived experience of peacebuilding. One of the interviewees that we spoke to indicated that they want to conduct an extensive research programme that delves into the idea of peace:

> To get to the bottom of this and how to maintain peace – this is what I would like to do and I don't have the money to do it... We need to understand that we cannot go forward without making some serious, basic headway. Not doing the palliative, cosmetic or temporary solutions.

The problem with this from a funder's perspective is that peace is not easily quantifiable: the measurement of peace it is not as straightforward as counting the number of women in a given military or security force, or the organisation of a given number of workshops. Peace is hard to fit into a matrix in the appendix of a National Action Plan; its indicators are often too amorphous to identify the precise activities and quarters of the financial year:

> [T]his is a challenge for us because some donors might be interested in peacebuilding, conflict prevention and conflict resolution, but others, they are more focused on infrastructure, education, and agriculture projects.

In many ways, infrastructure, education, and agriculture are much easier to measure and to report tangible outcomes, than peacebuilding, conflict prevention and conflict resolution. But this peace work is perhaps the most crucial aspect of the WPS Agenda.

Fifth, the increasing broadening of the agenda poses additional challenges for an already overstretched and under-resourced WPS civil society:

> [T]he WPS Agenda is so broad – from humanitarian assistance which some of the big INGOs are interested in, to using a gender analysis in military procurement, to funding women's peace groups, sexual exploitation and abuse, to preventing violent extremism – and it keeps growing. And then people say we have to bring in climate, domestic elements like murdered indigenous women and

girls. It's so huge – and it's about how we keep all of those agendas boiling at the same time. It's also a bit of a challenge for us.

It is invariably going to be easier for a large INGO with a multi-focus mandate to attract funding from multiple sources compared to a two-person on-the-ground operation, even if the latter might well be better positioned to understand the local context and respond to the needs of a community in crisis.

A consequence of this funding environment, as mentioned above, is that INGOs are competing with much smaller, local CSOs for the same pots of funding (Arutyunova 2018, p. 258); and 'these organizations oftentimes are also in competition with each other… in particular over funds', as one of our interviewees explained. Large international organisations tend to have the advantage of being better 'rehearsed in speaking "donor language" and meeting bureaucratic funding requirements' (Esplen 2013, p. 8; see also Hunt et al. 2015, p. 357) than are their local counterparts. Local CSOs are often 'unused to operating in the large-scale partnerships currently proliferating and favoured by international government donors' (Hunt et al. 2015, p. 355). As an interviewee explained,

> It [is] impossible for small organisations to compete with the whole world – we're already competing with bigger and well-financed international networks… I've also seen the professionalization of the WPS civil society field – some of our member organisations have made applications and haven't been able to get funds because they weren't seen as professional enough.

Another describes the inclusion of certain organisations and not others as a 'syndicate':

> And even… while working or organizing different activities like training or national plan action or implementation or any kind of things, they didn't even invite me. There is a syndicate. There is a syndicate of the – of the few people, few organisations… That is why the Women, Peace and Security agenda is very narrow in [redacted country] and it is not implemented… in reality.

This idea of professionalisation as a sort of 'signalling' practice – a form of 'we can talk the talk so you can trust us with the money' – has racialised and gendered implications. Is 'professional' code for 'doing it as the global minority does'? It also means moving from the private sphere – conventionally conceived of as a realm of the feminised informal – to the masculinised public sphere; the seemingly benign 'professionalisation' then becomes a sort of code for a Westernised masculinisation of civil society, even though the effectiveness of these spaces is often precisely that they are informal and grassroots in nature.

This professionalisation process takes different forms. As noted above, it can be about using the 'right' language. But it can also be administrative or strategic in nature, as a number of interviewees noted:

> The network needed to be formalised to allow for our international work... for logistics like setting up a bank account.

> We just recently went through a formalisation – we existed very informally, but [recently], we filed the papers to become a not-for-profit organisation.

> [T]he organisation has also been established for [a number of] years now, so the way we work has changed. We now have a strategy, which sets out our vision, our mission, our aim, our theory of change, and our objectives.

Professionalisation is not always a bad thing; opening a bank account, for example, may well be necessary for receiving and disbursing much-needed funds. However, we strongly argue that it is important to understand precisely what the criteria of 'professionalisation' are, and how they might operate to exclude certain actors – particularly those who are working on the ground in challenging contexts with limited resources or capacity to take on the onerous administrative requirements that often accompany external (and especially project-based) funding.

This process of professionalisation also creates a cycle: the INGOs that have more resources, greater institutional capacity and established relationships with donors (Hunt et al. 2015, p. 256) are inevitably more competitive in subsequent funding opportunities. Consequently, 'these spaces are increasingly inhabited by large, multi-mandate international development agencies, while local women's rights organisations without these characteristics remain marginalised from these processes' (Hunt et al. 2015, p. 356). This has created a hierarchy within civil society; as one of our interviewees explained:

> I mean, from where I sit... there's a big issue with the funding, which is likely to decrease in the future. And so that hierarchy

may have to do with the size of the organization. And if funding for smaller organizations is going down, you're going to see a worsening of the hierarchy and the space even further. And I mean it's not just WPS, it's civil society in general. That's the big worry.

As another noted:

The amount of money going in is very, very small. When we said as a network – what are our common asks? The one that always comes at the top of the list is funding for women peacebuilders: women-led organisations building peace... The scarcity model has been so prevalent, and the underfunding has been an incredible challenge to the whole sector, I think... Where is the money for the women's organisations who are doing this work? WPS funding writ large is important and has to grow, but so does the funding for the organisations doing the hard work, and has to grow as a percentage of what you're doing. Yes, great that you cut checks to the World Food Programme or the UNFPA, but that has to be accompanied by money for women-led women's rights organisations, feminist organisations. That's still a struggle for us here, to get people to understand the difference and to see that it's the funding for women's organisations that – everything else is essential and important, but that's really the heart of the matter.

Aside from creating a challenging work environment, we believe that the funding decisions that are made in this area are premised on the idea *that the work will be done anyway* – what Kate Bedford describes as the 'exhaustion solution' (2009, p. 22). As we discuss in Chapter 6, this is partly because of a feminist commitment to the cause and because of the social relational ties between some of the civil society actors working on WPS. But it is also *despite* the inadequate funding, a hostile political climate and the general sense of despair that many of the interviewees expressed to us, and which we discuss in the following chapter. On a more pragmatic level, though, for grassroots peacebuilders particularly, they don't really have a choice as to whether to do the work or not, as the other option is conflict: you do the work, or you watch your community, region, or country descend (back) into violence.

As a result, a significant proportion of the work done in this area is voluntary and done in addition to other employment. Here, we measure the expenditure of resources not only in terms of money, but also time:

> [I]t's a totally volunteer network – we have no staff, everyone does this in addition to their day jobs.

> [I]n terms of pure advocacy, I think most of that is actually sort of self-funded... [A]ll these people that come from these organizations, okay. They get authorization from the organization to go. But you know, we show up at the meetings and we don't get extra money for that. Now most of these people, you know, the organisations will say yes, is it important for you to go. The editing of our policy brief for our policy statements, our recommendations to the [government or funders], that all that is extra work that is done, you know, in the evening hours.

> [This group's work is] fully based on voluntary work, you know, unpaid labour... So we keep meeting every now and then, but that's usually a reaction to something that it's happening in the public discourse... But I feel there hasn't been really a strategy behind it because no one has time to work on it in a way.

An especially frustrating aspect of this is that the work that civil society does is recognised and seemingly valuable to governments and other funding bodies. Our research participants explained the extent to which governments see utility in their work:

> We have a very close relationship with the [redacted] government. They are eager to hear our criticisms and our critical voice – they need it, they ask for it. The only thing stopping us is our lack of capacity (time and resources) to be really critical and reflective in our recommendations.

> The interest at the political level has then helped to inform bureaucrats, the officials at the official level, who have reached out and asked us... They'll ask for comments on a document, and we have to say that we don't have the capacity – then that leads to some of the funding discussions.

> [T]he feedback was, yes, the Security Council work was very important. They just wanted us to do more, more briefings, more thematic briefings, more civil society briefings. More but no one was volunteering to give us extra budget.

The WPS resolutions, the statements made by states at the WPS Open Debate, and the National Action Plans all seemingly recognise the value of the work of civil society. The UN Secretary-General's reports acknowledge the importance of civil society; for example, in 'Special Measures for Protection from Sexual Exploitation and Abuse' (A/72/751, p. 13), the Secretary-General writes:

> Civil society and humanitarian organizations are essential partners in our efforts to address sexual exploitation and abuse, both on the ground and in policymaking. They are often on the frontlines of protecting and providing life-saving assistance to vulnerable communities, and are a critical interface between affected communities and the United Nations system, as they frequently assist affected individuals who report allegations of sexual exploitation and abuse.

All of the WPS resolutions acknowledge the role of civil society in the WPS Agenda (in UNSCR 1325 it is framed as 'local women's peace initiatives and indigenous processes for conflict resolution' at para 8(b)), including UNSCR 2122 (2013), which notes (emphasis added):

> the *critical contributions* of civil society, including women's organizations to conflict prevention, resolution and peacebuilding and in this regard the importance of sustained consultation and dialogue between women and national and international decision makers.

Many of the states who have delivered statements at the Open Debates have also expressed praise for civil society; this includes, to take just a handful of examples, Afghanistan (see, for example, S/PV.6877), Armenia (see, for example, S/PV.8079), Colombia (see, for example, S/PV.7938), Ethiopia (see, for example, S/PV.8514) and the Dominican Republic (see, for example, S/PV.8514). Similarly, states have used National Action Plans to acknowledge the work of civil society; including, for example, Iraq's (2014) 'National Action Plan for Implementation of the United Nation Security Council Resolution 1325 on Women, Peace and Security 2014–2018', the third Dutch plan, 'The Netherlands National Action Plan on Women, Peace and Security 2016–2019' (The Netherlands 2016) and Sierra Leone's (2010) 'The Sierra Leone National Action Plan for the Full Implementation of United Nations Security Council Resolutions 1325 (2000) & 1820 (2008)'. There is, therefore, a great disparity between the lavish praise heaped on civil society and the meagre funding made available to them to continue their work.

So, where does this leave civil society? WPS work is complex, multi-sited, and woefully undervalued. For every few drops of visible (often performative) funding – a few thousand dollars donated to a UN fund or invested in a consultation – there is a vast well of invisible support on which the agenda and its champions in the realm of formal politics relies. This all happens in the context of decreasing opportunities for meaningful civil society engagement, and the destructive professionalisation and formalisation of civil society space. These dynamics have squeezed out many actors who are deemed insufficiently 'expert' (read: professional and formal) in WPS and have created a hierarchy within civil society as well as between the formal and informal political domains, which could usefully be the focus of future research.

5 Despair

Working on the Women, Peace and Security (WPS) agenda can be particularly difficult sometimes. As we have already discussed, there are day-to-day challenges, including those relating to funding, workloads and priorities. There are also content-related challenges; this area of work has violence at the heart of it which brings with it what one interviewee described as an 'additional kind of emotional burden'; it requires 'additional work that you have to do externally, emotionally to survive working on it'. For many, this comes with the territory of working in civil society and trying to make a difference in difficult circumstances (for a compelling elaboration of this point, see Myrttinen 2018). The conversations we have had with civil society actors working on the agenda, however, have revealed something beyond these everyday and emotional obstacles, to a kind of despair, which causes a profound form of depletion as it affects mental health and wellbeing (Rai, Hoskyns, and Thomas 2014; Rai, True, and Tanyag 2019). There are three particular points of despair that we identified across the interviews: the hostile political climate within which WPS civil society actors currently operate, and its influence on the passing of resolutions 2467 and 2493 in 2019; the role of civil society briefers at the UN Security Council; and the 20th anniversary of UNSCR 1325.

In recent times, we have observed a political climate that is increasingly hostile to women's rights. This political climate has inhibited – and sometimes actively rolled back – progress on women's rights. The people that we spoke with highlighted the challenges posed by increasingly populist, nationalist and conservative governments:

> [W]ith the political climate turning to populist, nationalist and less international, and with less bilateral trends, we need to safeguard those spaces and keep doors open and watch out that our members and our partner organisations are safe.

[W]hen the conservative government was in power – that was a very difficult time for civil society, for women's organisations here... who lost a lot of funding, and for organisations working on global issues because of hostility of that government to progressive, feminist organisations.

And clearly, we have a trend towards more attacks on women's human rights activists. You've got more misogynistic political discourse globally. Some states of course are fighting back, but I don't know where that leaves the space. I think it's immensely political... [A]t a global level, it's still a very patriarchal model. And right now, there's some push back. Still, I don't know where it leaves us as the space is shrinking.

In many countries, civil society operates under very conservative political systems with, in the words of one research participant, a 'very strong, aggressive right'. One interviewee noted that the Trump administration's policies in particular proved challenging for civil society actors working in and with the United States:

I think one of the things that has changed on the US side, particularly with this [the Trump] administration, is that the evangelical, the Christian, the anti-abortion civil society organizations are very strong and have tried to really capture a lot of the debate on WPS and trying to steer the discussion into issues related to abortion... [O]f course, for this administration, this [WPS] is not the priority.... But I think a lot of us in the civil society sphere, we're hoping this government is not going to last. And we're trying to keep afloat and alive those mid-level people working in the different agencies. And we continue to collaborate with them.

The impact of these kinds of politics on the WPS agenda was laid bare in April 2019, when the UN Security Council passed resolution 2467. An early draft of this resolution made reference to women's 'sexual and reproductive health', which was designed to provide women who had experienced conflict-related sexual violence access to things like emergency contraception and HIV prevention and treatment. Even though access to termination of pregnancy was not explicitly mentioned, the United States, in keeping with its long-standing foreign policy dictates and the Trump administration's 'Global Gag Rule' (Skuster, Khanal, and Nyamato 2020), 'threatened to veto the resolution if it ensured access to reproductive and sexual healthcare' (Proctor 2019). As a result, the reference to 'sexual and reproductive health' was removed late in the negotiations in order to secure the US vote (with Russia and China abstaining). The clauses were instead replaced with 'a watered-down, reduced version of this language' (Allen and Shepherd 2019).

Similar concerns accompanied the passing of UNSCR 2493 in October 2019. This time, the issue arose around the lack of meaningful protection offered to women human rights defenders. During negotiations and in the 2019 Open Debate, China and Russia (both of whom ultimately abstained from voting) objected to the explicit mention of 'women human rights defenders'. According to the Russian delegation, this wording overstepped the mandate of the Security Council, while China stressed the concept of sovereignty. In the end, the specific wording of 'women human rights defenders' was left out of the resolution, and the final, adopted part now reads:

> encourages Member States to create safe and enabling environments for civil society, including formal and informal community women leaders, women peacebuilders, political actors, and those who protect and promote human rights, to carry out their work independently and without undue interference, including in situations of armed conflict, and to address threats, harassment, violence and hate speech against them.[1]

It is regrettable and deeply demoralising that UNSCR 2493 was not explicit in the need to protect women human rights defenders. People, especially women, working to defend human rights are at very real risk of increased repression, violence and impunity, including through defamation campaigns, judicial harassment and gender-based violence. As Bineta Diop explained in her briefing to the Security Council (in 2012 in meeting S/PV.6877):

> Due to their work exposing violence against women and other human rights violations, women's human rights defenders are exposed to threats, intimidation, violence and at times alienation from their own communities. Those in Afghanistan, the Democratic Republic of the Congo and throughout the Middle East often face serious personal risk and sometimes death.

The Special Rapporteur on Human Rights Defenders in his annual report to the Human Rights Council also reported a rise in 'misogynistic, sexist and homophobic speech' (2019, p. 6) by political leaders normalising targeted violence against women, women human rights defenders and gender non-conforming people.

Human rights defenders face persecution by both state and non-state actors. As one of our interviewees starkly explained:

> [Y]ou become a target of both the government and the conflicting parties. You also expose the life of your loved ones... the perpetrators will treat you as traitor... [and] at some level the government feels threatened with your work, you become vulnerable to forceful disappearance, torture, arrest and brutality.

In a similar vein, in 2017, Lisa Davis (on behalf of the NGO Working Group on Women and MADRE), told the Security Council (S/PV.7704):

> [S]peaking out about conflict-related sexual violence is extremely dangerous, especially in cases where State actors are implicated as perpetrators. Local activists who speak up about rape by security forces often face imprisonment, threats of rape and deliberate efforts to tar their reputations. Often impunity still reigns for those crimes. Under the guise of countering violent extremism, Governments around the world are invoking national security concerns to justify the systematic harassment, arrest and detention of women activists and providers. That securitized and militarized framework also contributes to the shrinking of civil society space. The efforts of the international community to address the threats of violent extremism cannot succeed while women's human rights defenders are under threat. As our colleagues engaging in the dangerous work of defending women's rights know, the bitter irony is that policymakers often speak to the importance of that work while doing little to support it in practice. From Syria to Afghanistan, Burundi and the Democratic Republic of the Congo, our brave colleagues continue to work in conflict zones, facing death threats and sometimes paying the ultimate price for their work.

In her 2014 briefing, Suaad Allami (representing the NGO Working Group on WPS and the Women for Progress Centre in Iraq) also shared insights about the human cost of violence against women's human rights defenders (S/PV.7289; see also Charo Mina-Rojas' briefing in S/PV.8079 of 2017 and cook 2016):

> I am here for my friends and colleagues Samira Salih Al-Nuaimi and Umaima Al-Jebara, who were recently killed defending

women's rights in Iraq; Razan Zaitouneh, who was abducted for documenting human rights violations in Syria; and all activists who risk their lives daily to make women and peace and security not just a resolution, but a reality.

Even just the perception that you are working on women's rights issues can expose civil society actors to harm; as a research participant noted:

> Unfortunately, we also accept that we cannot collaborate with an organisation... when it's too threatening for them to be in collaboration with us, or where there are ramifications for partners to be seen on our website. It is a hardening climate internationally. We still have contact with many parties and they always testify to this hardening climate for women's human rights defenders. We need to take more precautions today and work in a way that does not endanger activists or leaders and to maintain these spaces and recognise that they are important.

As Oliver Walton (2013) points out, organisations that receive funding from international donors can be seen as being the mouthpiece for foreign governments and therefore anti-national and a threat to sovereignty. While civil society actors on the ground face these attacks, so too do civil society representatives who brief the UN Security Council's WPS Open Debates.[2]

The WPS Open Debates began with the passing of UN Security Council Resolution 1325 and are held annually – usually in October, the anniversary month – with distinct but related debates on the issue of sexual violence in conflict held annually in April. The Open Debates are informed by the Secretary-General's annual report on Women, Peace and Security, and during the session the Council hears statements from briefers as well as member states. The briefers usually include the UN Secretary-General, the Executive Director of UN Women, representatives of other UN agencies, and most importantly, a civil society representative selected by the NGO Working Group on WPS.[3]

There are multiple sources of despair that stem from these civil society briefings. For one, the visibility of the civil society briefers has resulted in reprisals. As the Assistant Secretary-General for Human Rights (United Nations Human Rights Council 2020) reported:

> Over the past years, reported cases of intimidation and reprisals for cooperation with the UN have increased in both numbers and severity... We have documented cases of reprisals before, during

and after cooperation with the Security Council and its subsidiary bodies. We have seen intimidation, harassment and surveillance of partners in their country of origin or at UN Headquarters, online and offline. We have documented travel bans and interrogation before and after travel. We have also received information about detention and ill-treatment for cooperating with the Council.

As one person we spoke with pointed out to us:

Civil society representatives take great risks by briefing the Security Council. They are the ones sticking their necks out by talking about really difficult and often controversial issues. They are the ones who have to go back to their countries and continue working on these issues after having publicly raised them before the UN and Member States. Security Council members invite them to brief, and sometimes that is literally the extent of what they do... they're not even paying for these briefers or otherwise supporting them either during the briefing or after they brief.

These reports led to an Arria Formula Meeting on 'Reprisals against women human rights defenders and women peacebuilders who engage with the Security Council and its subsidiary bodies', co-organised by the Dominican Republic and the UK, and co-sponsored by Belgium, Estonia, and Germany, in February 2020. We are yet to see if there will be a tangible outcome from these reports, resolutions and meetings. Given the track record on the implementation of the WPS agenda thus far, though, there is reason to be sceptical.

Another form of related despair comes from the expectation that civil society speakers will frame their briefings in line with UN norms – which can curtail the voices of women and restrict the stories that can and cannot be told (and the ways in which they can and cannot be told). There is a sense that women are being rolled out to tell powerful and often personal stories, to little effect. Sheri Gibbings (2011) shows how even gender advocates within the UN system have to tread a careful line and in doing so sometimes limit freedom of expression. Gibbings recounts the experience of two Iraqi women, Amal Al-Khedairy and Nermin Al-Mufti, who, in 2003, were invited to UNIFEM (now UN Women) to speak informally with NGOs and representatives from member states and the UN (having not been given permission to speak formally before the Security Council). The organisers of the meeting, Gibbings reports, had expected Al-Khedairy and Al-Mufti 'to speak positively about women's efforts in the reconstruction of Iraq and the role the UN could play' (p. 524). That wasn't what happened. Instead, '[t]hey spoke in nationalist terms, condemned the invasion by the USA and UK as imperialist and critiqued the UN for its lack of support' (p. 524), with participants later 'labell[ing] their comments as "angry"' (2011, p. 524). They didn't stick to the script. They didn't show the deference to which their audience was accustomed. They broke the unspoken rules of 'speak[ing] in accordance with UN discourses (which presented women as peacemakers and emphasized that there was an important role for the UN to play in the reconstruction)' (2011, p. 525).

It was a known fact in meetings with Security Council members that NGOs were not allowed to make reference to specific Security Council members in ways that questioned their tactics or approaches to peace. Al-Khedairy and Al-Mufti's performance illustrated that powerful norms exist around the Women, Peace and Security agenda, and that certain performances could be anticipated and expected, while others were discouraged.

(Gibbings 2011, p. 525)

These constraints on voice and representation are not limited to UN contexts alone. The experience of Australian civil society representatives on the Australian Government's Inter-Departmental Working Group on Women Peace and Security echoes similar challenges. The Working Group was tasked with developing the second Nation Action Plan Women Peace and Security. Civil society representatives on the Working Group had to comply with confidentiality clauses which meant that, in effect, they could not share with their constituency how the plan was developing or what issues were contentious in order to mobilise for advocacy. A further despair was the devaluing of the local knowledge that civil society in Australia brought to the discussions. The Australian Government ultimately opted to hire international consultants instead of engaging local expertise to support the drafting of the plan. When local civil society expertise was sought, it was through a voluntary, unpaid community of practice – and by invitation only.

This brings us to a third source of despair: that nothing ever changes despite the briefings of life on the ground. As a consequence of this, there is a justifiably deep sense of cynicism and hopelessness. Why bother going to the Security Council, sharing your story and those of your fellow citizens, and potentially put yourself (and your family, friends, and colleagues) at risk of retaliation when nothing ever comes of it?

As Julienne Lusenge, the Director of the Congolese Women's Fund and the President of Solidarité Féminine pour la Paix et le Développement Integral, said when speaking for the second time before the Security Council (2015, S/PV.7533):

> Seven years ago, in 2008, I came to New York to speak in the Security Council. I described the conflict in my country, the Democratic Republic of the Congo. I set out in detail the sexual violence, murders and massacres. I came to ask for concrete action for the implementation of resolution 1325 (2000) and the integration of the fight against sexual violence in peacekeeping missions. Today, 15 years after the adoption of resolution 1325 (2000) and seven years after my first briefing to the Council, I am once again addressing this body. I thought long and hard before deciding to come back here, and wondered whether or not it was worth the effort.

One interviewee we spoke with expressed her concern that civil society briefers have become part of the institutional landscape where the visibility and performance of civil society engagement is seen as more important than substantive change in implementing the WPS agenda:

> Sometimes, you're going to have states saying, "Hey, how come there hasn't been a civil society speaker in May, or in June, when we had seven in April?" So it's positive that states are also becoming used to seeing civil society as part of the norm. But at the same time, inviting a civil society briefer is not an end in and of itself. The purpose of the briefings are the issues and otherwise unheard perspectives that they bring to a Security Council discussion. We need to start seeing their issues and recommendations reflected in the outcomes and the work of the Security Council. And I'm afraid that has not happened systematically as yet. So we must hold the Security Council to a higher standard. While it is great that they're inviting civil society briefers, we now want them to take on board what they're saying. Otherwise, there's the danger that civil society is going to be instrumentalized, and simply serve to check the boxes for even the most supportive member states.

The fear of instrumentalisation is linked to another despair: of being co-opted and exploited for political purposes in ways that undermine the independence of civil society. As in the case of the two briefers, Amal Al-Khedairy and Nermin Al-Mufti, in Sheri Gibbings' (2011) article and the experience of civil society representatives working on the Australian National Action Plan discussed above, there comes a time when civil society feels that more assertive tactics (such as naming and shaming) are required. But being a vocal critic can come at a price – that your seat at the table is taken away and given to those civil society organisations that are less outspoken (Van der Borgh and Terwindt 2014).

It is unsurprising given this backdrop – and the lack of meaningful implementation of the WPS agenda more broadly – that the civil society actors we spoke with were almost unanimously concerned about the direction in which the agenda is going and the twentieth anniversary of UNSCR 1325 in 2020. One reported being 'pessimistic'; another told us 'I am quite worried. I don't think things are going in the right direction'. One of the biggest frustrations is the proliferation of resolutions in the face of little action:

> As far as we can tell, everyone is saying 'resource and implement'; if the commitments were there and realised and really meaningfully implemented, then it would already create a huge difference – we don't need more commitments.

> And if you take all the UN documents. Fantastic. Everything is written, you know, it's all beautiful. But then the thing keeps on repeating itself.

Another fear is the increasing institutionalisation of the Agenda:

> 2020 feels daunting and a very sobering moment to take stock... of the progress that has been made and how WPS is being interpreted and implemented and what are all of the more classic questions around the massive drawbacks of having it housed somewhere at the UNSC as a formal resolution and how does that contradict a lot of the WPS-related advocacy and programming that was taking place well before 2000 through women's networks and movements, and in civil society. It feels worrying to think about it like that.

> I think that the kind of revolutionary impulse of Women, Peace and Security has been potentially dampened down.

The real hope for progressing the WPS Agenda doesn't seem to be coming from the UN or its Security Council:

> I think to get excited about 20 years... do we think the world is more peaceful, more secure? Probably not. Do we think the world is more feminist? Maybe. And this is why for me, teaching is so important because if I wasn't teaching and engaging with young people on this topic, I would feel hopeless all the time. So that's, where I get excited and that's where I feel inspired. But also I think... seeing the kind of work that people are actually doing on a day-to-day basis to act, to organize, to advocate, to, you know, fight against. So for me... [t]he excitement is with the work people are doing...

> There's the WPS of the UNSC and NAPs and that's one type, but there's also WPS that has been going on for decades that has been held and driven forward by feminist networks and movements around the world, and that is a really important space to protect and celebrate and sustain. That made me feel... we don't only need to see WPS through what the UNSC is or is not achieving, but there are ways of recognising work that's going on that's really good and there is progress being made.

Overwhelmingly, though, the conversations that we had evinced a deep scepticism about the actual commitment of states to the cause. They tended to see the 20th anniversary celebrations in particular, and the expression of support for the WPS agenda in general, largely as a public relations exercise by UN member states:

> It's not going to be a moment to celebrate the achievements of women and girls and civil society in an international context... I think it's going to feel very 'governments patting each other on the back'. It's more of a branding exercise for them.

> I'm very suspicious of any time we celebrate these kind of markers as you know, reaching some kind of massive achievement when we have to be really careful about what's actually happening and what's actually – you know, like the most recent passage or the most recent Security Council resolution, right? I think should make us all very scared about the kind of you know, the rolling back of the gains that have been made or the kinds of threats that do stand.

[E]ven states supportive of the WPS agenda often see WPS as an add-on rather than a core peace and security issue, and simply a way to bolster their progressive credentials rather than take an unpopular stand on protecting women's rights that might cost them political capital.

All the forms of despair we have discussed above – the hostile political climate, the risks, the hopelessness, and the well-founded cynicism – deplete. They represent the depletion of time, energy, and hope. As described in Chapter 3, the concept of depletion through social reproduction (Rai, Hoskyns, and Thomas 2014) represents an effort to capture the reduction or diminution of wellbeing and human capacity through social reproduction activities such as care. Depletion can thus be defined as 'the level at which the resource outflows exceed resource inflows in carrying out social reproductive work over a threshold of sustainability' (Rai, Hoskyns, and Thomas 2014, pp. 87–88). In the context of our analysis, we can identify depletion if the time, energy, and emotional investment required to do the WPS work exceed the time, energy and emotional resources available to do it – which seems often to be the case. And yet despite this depletion, despite the despair, the care labour continues unabated. It comes in the form of support and story-sharing:

> You know what happens is we live in small circles. It's the same women coming all the time and we talk to each other. It's very good. We, in our network, we call it group therapy, which is useful and which has been extremely beneficial if you want to talk to the women who have been engaged and who have gone – who are going or who have gone through this process before, or conflicts, whatever.

But it also comes in the form of radical hope despite grim times:

> It's hard to say what we hope for without contextualizing that hope within the political reality that we live in, because obviously, my hope is transformation. That we see a clear political shift in how these states think about women's rights and the WPS agenda.

Often, this despair is overwhelming. However, there seems to be one thing that keeps the work going, and this is a profound feminist commitment in the agenda. We turn to this dimension of care in the following chapter.

Notes

1. Note also that the General Assembly passed resolution 68/181, 'Promotion of the Declaration on the Right and Responsibility of Individuals, Groups and Organs of Society to Promote and Protect Universally Recognized Human Rights and Fundamental Freedoms: protecting women human rights defenders', in 2013.
2. The UN Security Council Open Debates represent an opportunity for the workings of the Security Council to be made open to the wider UN and the international community. Despite the moniker, however, Open Debates are not so much debates as they are an exchange of largely pre-prepared statements.
3. The first substantive WPS Open Debate took place on 25 July 2002 (S/PV.4589), with 26 states in attendance along with the Under-Secretary-General for Peacekeeping Operations, the Assistant Secretary-General and Special Adviser on Gender Issues and Advancement of Women and the Executive Director of the United Nations Development Fund for Women. The subsequent Open Debates followed the template set, including a growing number of states and various representatives from the United Nations – for example, in S/PV.4852 (29 October 2003), the Senior Gender Adviser of the United Nations Organization Mission in the Democratic Republic of the Congo delivered a briefing to the Security Council on the implementation of UNSCR 1325 on the ground in the DRC. The first briefer from civil society came in 2004, when Agathe Rwankumba, a lawyer and member of the Réseau des Femmes pour la Défense des Droits et la Paix (a non-governmental organisations based in the Democratic Republic of the Congo), was invited to participate in the October WPS Open Debate (S/PV.5066). She described the extensive gender-based violence in the DRC, and provided recommendations around funding, peacekeeping forces, and the ending of impunity. Since then, civil society briefers have represented a variety of thematic concerns and state-specific situations. They often share intensely personal stories of violence and loss and reiterate the important role of women in peace processes. The briefers have shared conflict experiences from Afghanistan, Côte d'Ivoire, Timor-Leste, Somalia, Libya, the Democratic Republic of the Congo, Mali, Uganda, Central African Republic, South Sudan, Nigeria, Iraq, Syria, Kurdistan, and Colombia. They have underlined the need for the meaningful implementation of UNSCR 1325; for sufficient financial resourcing for civil society to continue to do its work; and for the end of conflict, in all its forms. In UNSCR 2242 (2015), the Security Council also expressed an 'intention to invite civil society, including women's organizations, to brief the Council in country-specific considerations and relevant thematic areas' (para 5(c)). This is still a work in progress, but the first one took place in December 2016.

6   Commitment

As we noted in the previous chapters, funding creates significant challenges in this area of work and the current political climate, dangers inherent to the work, and lack of meaningful implementation of the agenda creates a great deal of despair and depletion. Given these trying circumstances, why do civil society actors keep showing up and doing the work? What emerged from the responses we received is a profound conviction in the agenda, and a deep commitment to feminist politics.

We didn't set out looking for this feminist commitment – what might be termed a feminist willfulness (see Ahmed 2014, 2017) – in the interviews. We knew from our friends, colleagues and acquaintances working in this area that it was a commonality that we shared, but we were unprepared to find the extent to which this commitment drives the agenda. It was variously described to us as 'sort of a labour of love' and 'a self-driven project in a lot of ways'; someone else described a sense of 'personal conviction'. One person told us: 'I believe in this subject. I believe what I do... [it's] meaningful and I feel very good about it'. Yet another explained that care is at the heart of their peacebuilding work:

> In our network, peacebuilding includes practicing love and care in times of need, separation, isolation, fear, and uncertainty... We are doing this because we care for our communities. Our initiatives are our language of care and love to remind each other that we are not alone.

For many people we spoke with, their work in Women, Peace and Security was borne not from a specific passion for the agenda (though that also exists); rather, people referred to their feminist politics as a key driver for doing this work.

> I've always [been] a feminist and I've happened to work in peace and security spaces... I know I've always [been] a feminist and I've been always looking for, you know, venues to practice feminism.

Indeed, some entered the WPS space with no specific intention to work on it. In many cases, it was seen as a means of pursuing a broader feminist project:

> [M]y drive has never been to work on the Women, Peace and Security agenda... I mean for me it's just – it's more: it's political, it's ethical. It's like it's driven by these kinds of anti-militarist, you know, like critical look at the securitization of... feminist agendas. That was my – that's always been my orientation before I even knew what Women, Peace and Security was.

> If you've seen with your own eyes how women in conflict-related situations are completely left out from the political game. If you've seen the actual local impact at an individual level, it stays with you and I think it makes you want to do something about it. So, of course, often yes, people want to make a difference. Then there are different ways of translating that into action and a meaningful engagement.

The WPS agenda is located in a broader field of work on peacebuilding, peacemaking, post-crisis resilience, and recovery; as such, it is not unusual for people working on WPS to be the only 'gender person' in their organisation. This adds to the emotional labour of making sure a gender lens is integrated into the organisation's work; but it also requires a deep personal commitment to putting feminist principles into practice and a willingness to fight for those principles on a daily basis:

> [I]n some organisations, I was the sort of gender person and it just felt that I had something to contribute in a way. And I also had a lot to learn because you can't just take all the gender theorising and simply plant [it] in essentially masculinist environments because it doesn't work that way. And, basically, everyone stops listening to you.

Sara Ahmed talks about this kind of work as 'pushy work' (2017, p. 107) – work that requires consistent and often protracted effort. 'The necessity of pushing', Ahmed explains, 'is a consequence of what has become hard or hardened over time... You have to push harder to dislodge what has become harder' (p. 109). Feminist killjoys are seen to create problems that were not there before (Ahmed 2017). This work is necessary work – but not necessarily fun work – when it is accompanied by disparaging sighs, eye rolls, and an audience that 'stops listening to you' (as one interviewee noted). It also brings with it its own kind of labour: a persistence in the face of resistance. But persistence takes effort. It takes time. It takes faith, and creativity. It is labour, it is tiring and it depletes.

This persistence is even more tiring (and tiresome) in light of WPS work often happening in addition to a person's 'official' role. In this case, WPS becomes an extra activity, driven by a personal conviction:

> [Work on WPS] was not happening and that was not my job when I started. I was hired to do a different job and I'm still doing that job. But I basically fundraised for it and led the way because I found it very strange that an organization working on armed conflict wouldn't incorporate this dimension into the work, because the civilians, you know, are 50:50 women and men. And given my background, I took it very personally to do something about it. So that's what happened.

> I think what worked really well was that it was a match between personal and organizational interests. So those people were very motivated to do this work and they were able to advocate within their organization why it's important though sometimes the interest has been already within the organization, but basically when it works really well, I feel it was a match.

The persistence also comes in the face of stigma and active resistance:

> [W]hether they listen to me or not, I keep doing, keep doing, keep doing. I keep doing, keep writing the articles in newspapers, books, keep doing research… I keep pushing even though they blame me, they challenge me; I am excluded, I don't have colleagues, but I keep pushing.

It is not surprising, therefore, that the feminist commitment to keeping the WPS agenda alive results in a heavy reliance on volunteer labour – to an extent that this has become an expectation both among governments and civil society organisations. As Charlotte Overgaard (2019, p. 129) points out, 'volunteering is the unpaid opposite of paid labour'. In other words, it is unpaid work. That a feminist commitment drives this work is laudable, but it is also undervalued.

It is also driven by a sense of 'if not me, then who?'. In the quote above, if it had not been for the person who was driven to do this work, it would not have been done. The idea that pushing the WPS agenda forward (or even just maintaining existing wins) relies solely on the goodwill and free labour of people is problematic and deeply concerning, and drives home the precarity and vulnerability of the gains made in WPS.

Much of the work around the WPS agenda is driven by relationships, and the nurturing and sustaining of these relationships are important dimensions of the reproductive labour undertaken by civil society organisations. These can be relationships with government actors, consultants, other civil society organisations, and individual activists, academics, and advocates. As funding is rarely sufficient to support relationship building, or to afford value to the time it takes to do this labour, relationships with government and other actors (including the UN entities, academic researchers, and private sector organisations) can be extractive and asymmetrical. Nonetheless, there is a huge amount of goodwill (driven in large part by the feminist commitment we identify above) across the sector that sustains the relational dimension of this reproductive labour.

One of the primary ways in which the WPS agenda is visibly implemented is through states' National Action Plans – essentially public-facing policy documents that lay out a state's WPS achievements to date and makes plans for the next handful of years. Voluntary work by civil society actors often bring the NAPs to life, and NAPs have proven to be a useful entry point for civil society organisations to establish a relationship with state actors. This willingness to volunteer to build community engagement around the WPS agenda represents another form of care labour – it represents 'hope labour'. The concept of hope labour is 'premised on the logic of investment'; the idea 'that exposure and experience will possibly lead to employment in the future' (Allan 2019, p. 66). In the case of civil society working on WPS, there is a hope that feminist commitment to mobilising might open up opportunities for accessing funding, but more importantly, it is the hope that this work can influence the commitments that governments make in their NAPs:

> Our main objective from the day it was set up was to influence the government's peace and security work. This includes everything from the National Action Plans to the broader peace and security to ensuring gender equality is part and parcel of those policies... We have had quite good access to government WPS officials but

that doesn't mean we're having influence on all peace and security policies from a WPS and gender equality perspective... But where are we not having access and influence and how can we try to change that?

Engagement around the development of NAPs has been through both formal meetings and informal conversations. The level of access, unsurprisingly, has varied from organisation to organisation; some reported being akin to the 'chosen' ones who felt that there was a meaningful and productive relationship with the government, which included small amounts of funding, invitations to events, and a genuine engagement and consultation with the organisation. Others, however, describe less effective relationships:

> You know, for the military, it's relatively simple. I make your manual and I tell them, you've got to do it. But for the political side of it, then all sorts of things, just sort of playing into the game and among other things that it's not necessarily... although I'll give a lot of, you know, good political lip service to it, it's not my major concern.

> We, from the civil society point of view, had wanted to have a more institutionalised way of consulting with the different agencies. We have had consultations, but they were always sort of informal. There was never a real formal mechanism whereby civil society and agencies could talk about these issues. Generally, the way it went is that the [redacted] would invite the agencies to come and brief them. And sometimes the agencies would ask for meetings with civil society to get some feedback on some of the things that they were working on.

The second key relationship that many we spoke with identified were with other WPS civil society organisations and actors. Sometimes these relationships are sought out and maintained for strategic reasons, generally because of access to different, and potentially valuable, networks:

> [O]ur member organisations – we are an umbrella organisation... and their networks are, of course, important – and those member organisations and their networks are sometimes sought out strategically. Recently, we recruited new member organisations that was not purely organic but also strategic in terms of their networks.

At other times, some spaces were identified as being specifically effective for potentially fruitful new collaborations:

> [W]e're going to visit the WPS week at the UN this year... We're expecting new connections to come out of that, by finding who is important, who we need to collaborate with, or be seen together with – who we should lend our voice to as well.

> I think we're quite reliant on multilateral processes to strengthen that kind of global community feeling – so things like the W7 conversations that happen ahead of the G7, have been spaces that my colleague have attended, and she came back from those feeling energised and asking "Why aren't there more opportunities for a formal global community?" Because it's so positive, and it's a shame that we only get to interact with each other when being funded to travel by states or organisations. I think in general, we find ourselves quite reliant on that – there are moments of global community building, but it doesn't feel very sustained.

Another aspect of this relationship-building amongst civil society organisations – who, again, are also frequently in competition when it comes to accesses the small pools of funding for WPS work – is to ensure the minimisation of any unnecessary duplication of work:

> We also keep in contact with [large organisation] to make use of their networks and to make sure that any overlaps in our work are constructive. It's the same with [other large organisation] and [third large organisation]. So those partnerships we strategically look for if we have an interest and it has been brought to our attention there is a need somewhere.

That said, there is something in these relationships beyond people engaging with one other purely professionally:

> A lot of the members have different international connections... and then we have relationships with some of the international networks like [redacted] – but they are often structured around personal relationships.

> I believe we do the same thing and we have the same values and yeah, I feel like there's lots in common.

> I would say these relationships came about quite organically as opposed to actively.

This shared philosophy – a shared feminist commitment – therefore seems to create particularly strong personal-professional hybrid networks which, in some senses, function as networks of care. A shared sense of pride, accomplishment and recognition of the work that civil society has done (and continues to do) unites people working on WPS, and underpins these relationships:

> I think even if you look even globally, not just in [redacted] but globally, you know, who has been driving this agenda it is in the first instance activist people who are personally engaged on the agenda. Those are the people who have made that this agenda has come so far and those are the people who've made that we now have [the] resolutions of the Security Council. Those are the people who have pushed for National Action Plans.

Despite this pride, some of our respondents identified having to dampen the feminist commitment when engaging with those who might not share the same political sympathies. Just like there is a 'professional' language around funding that appeals to funders, so too is there a way of speaking about the agenda to certain groups of people:

> [W]hen you talk with diplomats, you have to talk in a certain way. So we have people that we know are able to meet those standards and those norms and are not too "activisty" in a way.

Again drawing from Ahmed's work (2017), 'Decisions about words are decisions about usefulness: you use the words that are useful, the words that travel furthest, or that enable you to get a message through' (p. 98). Specifically in the context of UNSCR 1325, Sheri Lynn Gibbings has similarly noted (2011, p. 532):

> If language is power, then to use the same speech forms as the Security Council members allowed the NGO Working Group and UNIFEM to situate themselves on a similar playing field as Member States. Adopting the UN language norms situated these groups as worth listening to, which allowed them to push their agenda forward.

Nonetheless, the moral rage is there, if expressed to a more selective audience; as one of our interviewees explained:

> [T]here is a sort of moral rage, if you want, that gender inequalities still exist and that unequal gender structures continue to dictate policies. And I think for a lot of people and a lot of the

activists there is, you know, it's not just pure analytical thinking, but there's also a real moral engagement, I think.

Beyond the moral rage, feminist commitment also explains the frustration that results from the disparity between how the WPS agenda is conceptualised by civil society compared to by states and the United Nations. There is, in many ways, a fundamental disconnect between the two, with civil society actors often pushing for deep structural change, particularly around gender social norms and peace:

> We're really trying to put it as simply and clearly as possible that you can't work on many of the more "exciting" or animated parts of the WPS agenda without addressing the root causes and working on gender social norms and patriarchal systems and women and girls' economic empowerment in fragile and conflict contexts. So we're both looking at how to re-centre things like conflict prevention and women's participation and gender equality as important elements of gender equality, but also how to respond to the more buzzy things like CVE and how to have a position on that.

Nowhere is this divergence between civil society, on one side, and states and the UN on the other, more evident than when it comes to conflict prevention. The historical roots of the WPS agenda when traced back to the resolutions adopted by the International Congress of Women at The Hague, in 1915, call for an end to using war as means to resolve international disputes. The prevention of conflict has always been at the at the heart of WPS agenda. There is, of course, a political economy to conflict, manifest in the sale of weapons, political alliances, and displays of power (see, for example, Archer 2013). Countries like the UK, Sweden and the Netherlands, who have been vocal supporters of the WPS agenda, simultaneously profit handsomely from weapons manufacturing and arms export. Similarly, as the Australian Civil Society Coalition on Women Peace and Security (2018) pointed out to the Australian government in an open letter:

> The recent announcement of the Australian Government to increase defence exports, directly contributes to a proliferation of arms and a move towards increased militarisation. This is inconsistent with the Australian Government's commitment to the Women, Peace and Security Agenda.

We can by all means hold multiple truths, but these are untenable con-
tradictions that undermine any purported state support for the WPS
agenda. WPS civil society organisations find themselves constantly
reiterating a feminist vision of peace to states entrenched in a milita-
rised approach to peace and security:

> [W]e really had to go back to explain the narrative of 1325 being a
> conflict prevention agenda. And if the response from the Security
> Council is now just to add more women to the military, problem
> solved, then that's going to be really concerning.

> I think we need to focus more on disarmament and conflict preven-
> tion. Even when we talk about critical issues such as accountabil-
> ity, in some ways, it feels reactive. We're talking about the fact that
> war and violence exist, and what we need to do in order to address
> them properly and in line with human rights principles. We're not
> going to the core of the issue and saying, "Well, actually, WPS is
> really about opposing war, not sanitizing it." That's where femi-
> nists came from when the agenda was first conceived. We oppose
> war. We oppose intervention in the name of women's rights.

But once again, all of this commitment, all of this hope, all of the relationships, and the resistance: it is labour. It is work – and hard work at
that. It depletes those working in the WPS space, and should be both
recognised and remunerated.

7 Making 1325 work

In this book, we set out to make a relatively straightforward argument about the Women, Peace and Security (WPS) agenda and its conditions of success. As we explained in the introduction, at the outset of this project we didn't expect to focus on the work of civil society organisations directly; we thought that this was a project about the different ways in which WPS is being implemented across the world, an investigation of the variety of WPS practices and relationships with a view to better understanding the possibilities and limitations of the agenda itself. But time and again the conversations we were having with those involved in implementation, advocacy, and analysis of the WPS agenda in their disparate locations turned away from the practicalities of WPS work and took us into discussions of the affective and relational dimensions of that work. Interwoven with the accounts of how these dedicated practitioners were making the WPS agenda work were stories of how it made them feel, why they were devoting such time and energy to the project of realising the goals of 1325, and the demands of their commitment to the agenda. And at the heart of all these stories was care.

Participating in these conversations, listening back through the recordings, reading back through the transcripts, and returning repeatedly to the literature on women's civil society engagement in the WPS agenda, the idea that the success of the agenda itself is contingent on the care labour of civil society began to take shape. As we outlined in Chapter 2, the history of the agenda is a history of civil society activism devoted to upholding women's rights in conflict and conflict-affected settings, to realising women's empowerment and meaningful participation in peace and security governance, and ultimately to transforming the relations of the international system to nurture peace through effective and inclusive conflict prevention. Civil society organisations have been intimately involved in the development and implementation of the agenda from the very beginning, and so the commitment of these organisations – along with the expertise they bring to bear on the issues with which the agenda is concerned – is evident. While there is research evaluating the effectiveness of civil society engagement, and documenting the ways in which civil society continues to be involved in realising the principles of the agenda, there is little attention paid to the labour itself, and how it functions in the production and reproduction of the agenda, to make resolution 1325 work.

Thus, in Chapter 3, we turned to feminist political economy for conceptual inspiration to help us think through how to focus in an analytically productive way on the labour of civil society organisations that we interpret as a manifestation of care. Feminist political economists were the first to acknowledge that gendered relations of care are a form of social reproduction, which in turn is an essential component of formal economic activity: there can be no productive economy without a reproductive economy, and the division of labour in both spheres is profoundly gendered. We argue that the gendered stereotypes and attachments that associate social reproduction and care with femininity are echoed in the organisation of WPS labour; civil society organisations have become (or, really, been made) responsible for a significant volume of reproductive labour, taken on out of a commitment and care for the agenda's vision and values, without which the agenda would not be able to function. The care labour of civil society is a condition of the WPS agenda's success.

Continuing to draw inspiration from feminist political economists, we then used this theory to inform our analysis of the interviews we had conducted. The interview data revealed three dominant themes or dimensions of care: finding funding, dealing with despair, and maintaining a feminist commitment. The funding issue, which we explored in Chapter 4, relates explicitly to the political economy of WPS work. In the absence of consistent, reliable funding, civil society organisations are forced to navigate between two equally unsatisfactory imperatives: the need to devote time and energy to finding funding, on the one hand, to support those activities which absolutely require investment; and the need to take on significant amounts of unpaid work, on the other hand, to keep on with WPS work in the absence of material support. We draw out the impact of this persistent under-resourcing on civil society activities of, and affective engagement with, the agenda. We argue that the success of the agenda relies on a vast well of invisible support, which is not a sustainable arrangement in the long term and certainly puts into question the proclamation of commitments of support for the agenda by states: actual commitment must manifest in material resources that enable civil society organisations to continue – and be properly acknowledged and valued for – their WPS work.

The second dimension of care we explore relates to the ability of civil society organisations to keep going in the face of such a debilitating lack of resources. In Chapter 5, we drew on the concept of depletion, another vital contribution from feminist political economy which explains the emotional and physical effects of sustained reproductive labour that is unrecognised, under-valued, and under-resourced. In addition to the physical exhaustion of working long days, often taking on WPS work 'out of hours' or in addition to other tasks, civil society representatives talked to us about the emotional exhaustion of perpetually dealing with precarity and despair, which takes its own kind of toll. We identify a number of forms that depletion takes: the exhaustion of working against the grain in a hostile political climate; the worry of taking political risks and risking personal safety to defend women's rights; the toll that it takes emotionally working through hopelessness and despair; and the continued demands for resilience despite well-founded cynicism about the possibilities and limitations of the agenda.

The discussion we presented in Chapter 6 shows how the civil society representatives that we spoke to have found ways to replenish the emotional and physical reserves that are depleted by the care work they do. The primary source of emotional nourishment was found in the relationships developed with other, similarly positioned, activists and advocates, sustained by shared goals. The maintenance of a feminist commitment to the agenda, and the commitment to showing up and doing the necessary work to keep the agenda going, is the third and final dimension of care labour that we identify. It is constituted in the fractious, divided, but also dedicated and inclusive community of civil society organisations that do WPS work, and it is – as with the other dimensions we discuss – barely recognised as a condition of the agenda's success. There are, of course, tensions between the priorities of various civil society organisations, and there are certainly fraught relationships with government agencies in many places, such that the feminist commitment of WPS civil society organisations is constructed as an inhibitor to the success of the agenda rather than an enabler. But the motivation of care labour by the commitment to peace, justice, and transformation is, frequently, what keeps the agenda alive.

Although we have offered only a small sample of stories from civil society in this short book, we know that these stories resonate with many involved in this work. When we presented preliminary findings at a seminar towards the end of 2020, we were contacted by numerous people doing WPS work who wanted to tell us that they identified with our conclusions, they felt *seen* by the work we were doing, and that they wanted to talk more, and more openly, about doing the work that they do and the impact that it has. We have drawn out only a few dimensions of care labour in our analysis, and we are sure that there are many more to be explored. Collaborative research with civil society organisations – properly compensated, and co-designed – would potentially be a productive way to extend the analysis we have presented here. Further, presumably there are other spheres in which the same dynamics are visible: where care labour of civil society is a condition of success. It would also be interesting to see whether the theoretical framework is useful in other issue areas or policy contexts beyond the WPS agenda.

In closing, we want to acknowledge that there are, of course, potential concerns to be raised about theorising women's peace work as care labour, as drawing on theories of social reproduction risks naturalising the work that civil society organisations do in service of the WPS agenda. The difficulties here are twofold. First, in the same way that care labour in the domestic realm is still persistently presumed to be 'natural' and is therefore consistently unappreciated and underfunded, our analysis might serve to reinforce the idea that it is only 'natural' that the social movements that mobilised in support of the agenda in the first place would take on this under-valued and under-resourced labour. Second, and more perniciously, presenting the care labour of civil society as a condition of the agenda's success risks attributing responsibility for shortcomings to those under-valued and under-resourced organisations. These concerns are legitimate, and we accept that there are no straightforward resolutions to the problems that these concerns pose. In the same way as advocating for the meaningful participation of women in peace processes risks reinforcing stereotypes of women as peacemakers, there is a need to work within the structures of gendered power even as we seek to challenge them. What this research has shown us is that those doing WPS work – in policy environments, civil society, academia, and beyond – are creative, critically minded, and well able to navigate these tensions.

In this project, we set out to consider the varieties of WPS work being undertaken across the world. We ended up investigating the motivations, pressures and frustrations experienced by WPS civil society actors, as well as the goals and challenges. We have put forward here a very simple proposition: that the care labour of civil society is a condition of the WPS agenda's success. Without the initial efforts of civil society, there would be no WPS agenda; without the continued labour and care of these organisations, the agenda could not be realised. But the supply of this labour is not inexhaustible, and the continued practices of care have a cost. Realising the agenda requires a proper accounting of care and commitment, a thorough-going evaluation of the resources that are demanded to support in the ongoing reproduction of the agenda not just in dollar amounts in national budgets but in the time, energy, and emotional labour invested by civil society organisations. Rai, Hoskyns, and Thomas (2014, pp. 98–100) outline three inter-linked strategies to remediate depletion through social reproduction in the economic sphere, and we might learn from these valuable insights to shift the needle on debates about WPS resourcing: strategies of mitigation (individual initiatives to share the cost of social reproduction more equitably), replenishment (the investment of resources that reduce the cost of social repro-duction), and transformation (restructuring relations of power that shape how social reproduction is valued). At the heart of these strat-egies is a commitment to reckoning with the value of reproductive labour, and the effect that it has on those who are expected to bear its cost. Just as feminist political economists have taught us to identify and acknowledge the dynamics of social reproduction without which formal economic activity would not be possible, it is long past time that civil society organisations receive the recognition and investment they so deserve.

Bibliography

Australian Civil Society Coalition on Women, Peace and Security (2018) 'Advocacy letter to the Prime Minister', http://wpscoalition.org/wp-content/uploads/2018/05/Letter-to-the-PM-from-the-Australian-Civil-Society-Coaltion-on-Women-Peace-and-Security.pdf

Ahmed, Sara (2017) *Living a Feminist Life*, USA: Duke University Press.

Ahmed, Sara (2014) *Willful Subjects*, USA: Duke University Press.

Allan, Kori (2019) 'Volunteering as hope labour: The potential value of unpaid work experience for the un- and under-employed', *Culture, Theory and Critique*, 60(1): 66–83.

Allen, Louise and Laura J. Shepherd (2019) 'In pursuing a new resolution on sexual violence Security Council significantly undermines women's reproductive rights', https://blogs.lse.ac.uk/wps/2019/04/25/in-pursuing-a-new-resolution-on-sexual-violence-security-council-significantly-undermines-womens-reproductive-rights/

Archer, Colin (2013) 'Military spending and the UN's Development Agenda', *Peace Review*, 25(1): 24–32.

Arutyunova, Angelika (2018) 'Beyond investing in women and girls: Why sustainable long-term support to women's rights organizations and movements is key to achieving women's rights and gender equality', 247–271 in Zohra Khan and Nalini Burn (eds), *Financing for Gender Equality: Realising Women's Rights Through Gender Responsive Budgeting*, Basingstoke: Palgrave Macmillan.

Bakker, Isabella (2007) 'Social reproduction and the constitution of a gendered political economy', *New Political Economy*, 12(4): 541–556.

Barrow, Amy (2009) '[It's] like a rubber-band': Assessing UNSCR 1325 as a gender mainstreaming process', *International Journal of Law in Context*, 5(1): 51–68.

Basu, Soumita, Paul Kirby, and Laura J Shepherd (eds) (2020) *New Directions in Women, Peace and Security*, Bristol: Bristol University Press.

Bedford, Kate (2008) 'Governing intimacy in the World Bank', 84–106 in Shirin M. Rai and Georgina Waylen (eds) *Analysing and Transforming Global Governance: Feminist Perspectives*, UK: Palgrave Macmillan.

Bedford, Kate (2009) *Developing Partnerships: Gender, Sexuality and the Reformed World Bank*, Minneapolis and London: University of Minnesota Press.

Benería, Lourdes and Gita Sen (1981) 'Accumulation, reproduction, and "Women's Role in Economic Development": Boserup revisited', *Signs: Journal of Women in Culture and Society*, 7(2): 279–298.

Benería, Lourdes (1979) 'Reproduction, production and the sexual division of labour', *Cambridge Journal of Economics*, 3(3): 203–225.

Björkdahl, Annika and Johanna Mannergren Selimovic (2019) 'WPS and civil society', 428–438 in Sara E. Davies and Jacqui True (eds), *The Oxford Handbook of Women, Peace and Security*, Oxford: Oxford University Press.

Black, Anthony (2001) 'Concepts of civil society in pre-modern Europe', 33–38 in Sudipta Kaviraj and Sunil Khilnani (eds), *Civil Society: History and Possibilities*, Cambridge: Cambridge University Press.

van der Borgh, Chris and Carolijn Terwindt (2014) *NGOs Under Pressure in Partial Democracies*, London: Palgrave Macmillan.

Boserup, Esther (1970) *Women's Role in Economic Development*, London: George Allen Unwin Press.

Brodie, Janine (2003) 'Globalization, in/security, and the paradoxes of the social', 47–65 in Isabella Bakker and Stephen Gill (eds), *Power, Production and Social Reproduction: Human In/Security in the Global Political Economy*, Basingstoke: Palgrave.

Burkart, Christian, Tina Wakolbinger, and Fuminori Toyasaki (2018) 'Funds allocation in NPOs: The role of administrative cost ratios', *Central European Journal of Operations Research*, 26(2): 307–330.

Cabrera-Balleza, Mavic (2011) 'It is time to walk the talk and fulfil the promise of UNSCR 1325', *Palestine–Israel Journal of Politics, Economics, and Culture*, 17(3), https://pij.org/articles/1366/it-is-time-to-walk-the-talk-and-fulfill-the-promise-of-unscr-1325

Charlesworth, Hilary and Christine Chinkin (2013) 'The new United Nations gender architecture: A room with a view?', 1–60 in Armin von Bogdandy, Anne Peters, and Rüdiger Wolfrum (eds), *Max Planck Yearbook of International Law*, vol. 17, Leiden: Koninklijke Brill NV.

Cockburn, Cynthia (2007) *From Where We Stand: War, Women's Activism and Feminist Analysis*, London: Zed Books.

Cohn, Carol (2017) 'Beyond the "Women, Peace and Security" agenda: Why we need a feminist roadmap for sustainable peace', *Consortium on Gender, Security, and Human Rights*, http://genderandsecurity.org/sites/default/files/Cohn_-_Beyond_the_Women_Peace_and_Security_Agenda_Why_We_Need_a_Feminist_Roadmap_for_Sustainable_Peace.pdf.

Cohn, Carol, Helen Kinsella, and Sheri Gibbings (2004) 'Women, Peace and Security: Resolution 1325', *International Feminist Journal of Politics*, 6(1): 130–140.

cook, sam (2009) 'Security Council resolution 1820: On militarism, flashlights, raincoats, and rooms with doors – A political perspective on where it came from and what it adds', *Emory International Law Review*, 23(1): 125–140.

cook, sam (2016) 'The 'woman-in-conflict' at the UN Security Council: A subject of practice', *International Affairs*, 92(2): 353–372.

Coomaraswamy, Radhika et al. (2015) 'Preventing Conflict, Transforming Justice, Securing the Peace: A Global Study on the Implementation of United Nations Security Council Resolution 1325', http://peacewomen.org/sites/default/files/UNW-GLOBAL-STUDY-1325-2015%20(1).pdf

Davies, Sara E. and Jacqui True (eds) (2019) *The Oxford Handbook of Women, Peace and Security*, Oxford: Oxford University Press.

Douglas, Sarah and Cécile Mazzacurati (2017) 'Financing for gender-responsive peacebuilding: Setting financial targets as a tool for increasing women's participation in post-conflict recovery', 227–246 in Zora Khan and Nalini Burn (eds), *Financing for Gender Equality: Realising Women's Rights Through Gender Responsive Budgeting*, Basingstoke: Palgrave Macmillan.

El-Bushra, Judy (2007) 'Feminism, gender, and women's peace activism', *Development and Change*, 38(1): 131–147.

Esplen, Emily (2013) *Leaders for Change: Why Support Women's Rights Organisations?*, Womankind Worldwide, https://www.empowerwomen.org/en/resources/documents/2014/11/leaders-for-change-why-support-womens-rights-organisations?lang=en

Esplen, Emily, and Patti O'Neill (2017) 'From commitment to action: Aid in support of gender equality and women's rights in the implementation of the sustainable development goals', 205–225 in Zohra Khan and Nalini Burn (eds), *Financing for Gender Equality: Gender, Development and Social Change*, Basingstoke: Palgrave Macmillan.

Freeman, Scott and Mark Schuller (2020) 'Aid projects: The effects of commodification and exchange', *World Development*, 126.

Gibbings, Sheri Lynn (2011) 'No angry women at the United Nations: Political dreams and the cultural politics of United Nations Security Council resolution 1325', *International Feminist Journal of Politics*, 13(4): 522–538.

Griffin, Penny (2010) 'Gender, governance and the global political economy', *Australian Journal of International Affairs*, 64(1): 86–104.

Hamilton, Caitlin, Jordan McSwiney, Nyibeny Gum Naam and Laura J. Shepherd (2021) 'The social life of the Women, Peace and Security agenda: A digital social network analysis', *Global Society*, https://doi.org/10.1080/13600826.2021.1875996

Hamilton, Caitlin, Nyibeny Naam, and Laura J. Shepherd (2020) 'Twenty years of Women, Peace and Security National Action Plans: Analysis and Lessons Learned', https://www.lse.ac.uk/women-peace-security/assets/documents/2020/Twenty-Years-of-Women-Peace-and-Security-National-Action-Plans.pdf

Hans, Asha and Swarna Rajagopalan (eds) (2016) *Openings for Peace: UNSCR 1325, Women and Security in India*, New Delhi: SAGE.

Heathcote, Gina (2011) 'Feminist politics and the use of force: Theorising feminist action and Security Council resolution 1325', *Socio-Legal Review*, 7: 23–43.

Heathcote, Gina (2012) 'Naming and shaming: Human rights accountability in Security Council resolution 1960 (2010) on Women, Peace and Security', *Journal of Human Rights Practice*, 4(1): 82–105.

Heathcote, Gina (2018) 'Security Council resolution 2242 on Women, Peace and Security: Progressive gains or dangerous development?, *Global Society*, 32(4): 374–394.

Hill, Felicity, Mikele Aboitiz, and Sara Poehlman-Doumbouya (2003) 'Nongovernmental organizations' role in the build-up and implementation of Security Council resolution 1325', *Signs: Journal of Women in Culture and Society*, 28(4): 1255–1269.

Hochschild, Arlie (2000) 'Global care chains and emotional surplus value', 130–146 in Anthony Giddens and Will Hutton (eds) *On the Edge: Living with Global Capitalism*, London: Jonathan Cape.

Hoskyns, Catherine (2008) 'Governing the EU: Gender and macroeconomics', 107–128 in Rai Georgina (ed.), *Global Governance: Feminist Perspectives*, Basingstoke: Palgrave.

Hoskyns, Catherine, and Shirin M. Rai (2007) 'Recasting the global political economy: Counting women's unpaid work', *New Political Economy*, 12(3): 297–317.

Hunt, Abigail, Hannah Bond, and Ruth Ojiambo Ochieng (2015) 'Bridging inequalities through inclusion: Women's rights organisations as the "missing link" in donor government-led participatory policy development and practice', *Gender & Development*, 23(2): 347–364.

James, E. C (2010) *Democratic Insecurities: Violence, Trauma, and Intervention in Haiti*, Berkeley: University of California Press.

Jonjić-Beitter, Andrea, Hanna Stadler, and Flora Tietgen (2020) 'Civil society and its role within UNSCR 1325 National Action Plans', 177–199 in Manuela Scheuermann and Anja Zürn (eds), *Gender Roles in Peace and Security*, Cham: Springer.

Keane, John (1989) *Democracy and Civil Society*, London: Verso.

Keane, John (2010) 'Civil society, definitions and approaches', 461–464 in Helmut K. Anheier and Stefan Toepler (eds), *International Encyclopedia of Civil Society*, New York: Springer-Verlag.

Khan, Zohra (2017) 'Politics, policies and money: Delivering the Sustainable Development Goals for women', 177–203 in Zohra Khan and Nalini Burn (eds) *Financing for Gender Equality: Realising Women's Rights through Gender Responsive Budgeting*, UK: Palgrave Macmillan.

Kirby, Paul and Laura J. Shepherd (2020) 'Women, Peace and Security: Mapping the (re)production of a policy ecosystem', *Journal of Global Security Studies*, https://doi.org/10.1093/jogss/ogaa045.

Koester, Diana, Emily Esplen, Karen Barnes Robinson, Clare Castillejo, and Tam O'Neil (2016) 'How can donors improve their support to gender equality in fragile settings? Findings from OECD research', *Gender & Development*, 24(3): 353–373.

Kumar, Krishan (1993) 'Civil society: An inquiry into the usefulness of an historical term', *British Journal of Sociology*, 44(3): 375–395.

Kofman, Eleonore (2012) 'Rethinking care through social reproduction: Articulating circuits of migration', *Social Politics: International Studies in Gender, State & Society*, 19(1): 142–162.

Lecy, Jesse D., and Elizabeth Searing (2015) 'Anatomy of the nonprofit starvation cycle: An analysis of falling overhead ratios in the nonprofit sector', *Nonprofit and Voluntary Sector Quarterly*, 44(3): 539–563.

Manchanda, Rita (ed.) (2017) *Women and Politics of Peace: South Asia Narratives on Militarization, Power, and Justice*, New Delhi: SAGE.

Miller, Barbara, Milad Pournik and Aisling Swaine (2014) 'Women in Peace and Security through United Nations Security Resolution 1325: Literature Review, Content Analysis of National Action Plans, and Implementation', https://www.peacewomen.org/assets/file/NationalActionPlans/miladpournikanalysisdocs/igis_womeninpeaceandsecuritythroughunsr1325_millerpournikswaine_2014.pdf

Mundkur, Anu and Laura J. Shepherd (2018) 'Civil society participation in women, peace and security governance: Insights from Australia', *Security Challenges*, 14(2): 83–103.

Myrttinen, Henri (2018) 'Vignette 2: Packing for Kabul', in Althea-Maria Rivas and Brendan Ciarán Browne (eds), *Experiences in Researching Conflict and Violence: Fieldwork Interrupted*, Bristol: Polity Press.

Naraghi Anderlini, Sanam (2019) 'Civil society's leadership in adopting 1325 resolution', 38–52 in Sara E Davies and Jacqui True (eds), *The Oxford Handbook of Women, Peace and Security*, Oxford: Oxford University Press.

Naraghi Anderlini, Sanam (2007) *Women Building Peace: What They Do, Why It Matters*, Boulder, CO: Lynne Rienner.

Nwangwu, Chikodiri and Christian Ezeibe (2019) 'Femininity is not inferiority: Women-led civil society organizations and "countering violent extremism" in Nigeria', *International Feminist Journal of Politics*, 21(2): 168–193.

Olsson, Louise and Theodora-Ismene Gizelis (2013) 'An introduction to UNSCR 1325', *International Interactions*, 39(4): 425–434.

Otto, Dianne (2010) 'Power and danger: Feminist engagement with international law through the UN Security Council', *Australian Feminist Law Journal*, 32(1): 97–121.

Overgaard, Charlotte (2019) 'Rethinking volunteering as a form of unpaid work', *Nonprofit and Voluntary Sector Quarterly*, 48(1): 128–145.

Peterson, V. Spike (2002) 'Rewriting (global) political economy as reproductive, productive, and virtual (Foucauldian) economies', *International Feminist Journal of Politics*, 4(1): 1–30.

Proctor, Hannah (2019) 'Abortion in the WPS agenda: Is it time?', *WIIS*, https://www.wiisglobal.org/abortion-in-the-wps-agenda-is-it-time/

Peterson, V. Spike (2003) *A Critical Rewriting of Global Political Economy Integrating Reproductive, Productive, and Virtual Economies*, London: Routledge.

Pinter, Frances (2001) 'Funding of global civil society organisations', in Helmut Anheier, Marlies Glasius, and Mary Kaldor (eds), *Global Civil Society*, Oxford: Oxford University Press.

Porter, Elisabeth (2003) 'Women, political decision-making, and peace-building', *Global Change, Peace & Security*, 15(3): 245–262.

Rai, Shirin M., Catherine Hoskyns, and Dania Thomas (2014) 'Depletion: The cost of social reproduction', *International Feminist Journal of Politics*, 16(1): 86–105.

Rai, Shirin M., Jacqui True, and Maria Tanyag (2019) 'From depletion to regeneration: Addressing structural and physical violence in post-conflict economies', *Social Politics: International Studies in Gender, State & Society*, 26(4): 561–585.

Reimann, Kim (2006) 'A view from the top: International politics, norms and the worldwide growth of NGOs', *International Studies Quarterly*, 50(1): 45–67.

Safi, Mariam (2016) 'Afghan women and countering violent extremism: What are their roles, challenges and opportunities in CVE?, 118–140 in Naureen Chowdhury Fink, Zeiger Sara, and Bhulai Rafia (eds), *In A Man's World? Exploring the Roles of Women in Countering Terrorism and Violent Extremism*, Abu Dhabi: Hedayah and the Global Center on Cooperative Security.

Sauer, Birgit and Otto Penz (2017) 'Affective governmentality: A feminist perspective', 39–58 in Christine Hudson, Malin Rönnblom, and Katherine Teghtsoonian (eds), *Gender, Governance and Feminist Analysis: Missing in Action?* London: Routledge.

Shepherd, Laura J. (2008) *Gender, Violence and Security: Discourse as Practice*, London: Zed Books.

Shepherd, Laura J. (2017) *Gender, UN Peacebuilding, and the Politics of Space: Locating Legitimacy*, New York: Oxford University Press.

Shepherd, Laura J (2021) *Narrating the Women, Peace and Security Agenda: Logics of Global Governance*, New York: Oxford University Press.

Sierra Leone (2010) 'The Sierra Leone National Action Plan for the Full Implementation of United Nations Security Council Resolutions 1325 (2000) & 1820 (2008)', https://www.wpsnaps.org/app/uploads/2019/09/Sierra-Leone-NAP-2010.pdf

Singh, Shweta (2017) 'Re-thinking the 'normative' in United Nations Security Council resolution 1325: Perspectives from Sri Lanka', *Journal of Asian Security and International Affairs*, 4(2): 219–238.

Skjelsbæk, Inger and Torunn L. Tryggestad (2019) 'Donor states delivering on WPS: The case of Norway', 516–527 in Sara E Davies and Jacqui True (eds), *The Oxford Handbook of Women, Peace and Security*, Oxford: Oxford University Press.

Skuster, Patty, Ram Chandra Khanal, and Ernest Nyamato (2020) 'Relics of imperialism: US foreign policy on abortion in the COVID era', *Sexual and Reproductive Health Matters*, 28(3): 1–4.

Spurk, Christoph (2010) 'Understanding civil society', 3–28 in Thania Paffenholz (ed.), *Civil Society and Peacebuilding: A Critical Assessment*, Boulder: Lynne Rienner.

Steffek, Jens and Maria Paola Ferretti (2009) 'Accountability or "good decisions"? The completing goals of civil society participation in international governance', *Global Society*, 23(1): 37–57.

The Netherlands (2016) '*The Netherlands National Action Plan on Women, Peace and Security 2016–2019*', https://www.wpsnaps.org/app/uploads/2019/09/Netherlands-NAP-3-2016-2019.pdf

United Nations Human Rights Council (2020) 'ARRIA formula meeting of the Security Council by Ilze Brands Kehris on "Reprisals against women human rights defenders and women peacebuilders who engage with the Security Council and its subsidiary bodies": Statement by Assistant Secretary-General for Human Rights', 21 February 2020, https://www.ohchr.org/EN/HRBodies/HRC/Pages/NewsDetail.aspx?NewsID=25595&LangID=E

Vaittinen, Tiina, Amanda Donahoe, Rahel Kunz, Silja Bára Ómarsdóttir, and Sanam Roohi (2019) 'Care as everyday peacebuilding', *Peacebuilding*, 7(2): 194–209.

Yeates, Nicola (2004) 'Global care chains', *International Feminist Journal of Politics*, 6(3): 369–391.

Yeates, Nicola (2009) *Globalizing Care Economies and Migrant Workers: Explorations in Global Care Chains*, UK: Palgrave Macmillan.

Walton, Oliver (2013) '"Everything is politics": Understanding the political dimensions of NGOs legitimacy in conflict-affected regions', 19–39 in Rajeswary Ampalavanar Brown and Justin Pierce (eds), *Charities in the Non-Western World: The Development and Regulation of Indigenous and Islamic Charities*, Abingdon: Routledge.

Index

Note: Page numbers followed by 'n' refer to notes.

9780367642778